MW00878637

# Discovery of Self

## Answers to Inquiries of the God Seeker

Bryan & Wendy,

The choir of angels surround the loving work of humanity you do.

Love & Infinite Blessings of the Sehaji Masters,

Sr. Michael

# Discovery of Self

## Answers to Inquiries of the God Seeker

Michael Edward Owens

OPEN HEART BOOKS

*Editorial supervision by Michael Edward Owens*

*Editing and Publishing Team*

- *Cover Design: John Allen, Marcia Diane, Brett Marshall and Leslie Owens*
- *Editors: Jo-Ann Price, Matt Silver, Ann Sullivan, and Percy Walcott*
- *Graphics Support: Brett Marshall*
- *Indexing: Phyllis Brown and Dan Scott*
- *Publishing: Victor Cebollero, Carmen Roman-Cebollero, and Rich Price*



ISBN: 1-4196-9719-6
Library of Congress Control Number: TXu001003322

To order additional copies, please contact BookSurge Publishing:
www.booksurge.com 1-866-308-6235 orders@booksurge.com or Amazon.com

# Table of Contents



♥ ♥ ♥

# Introduction

Upon careful reflection and examination of my life, I found myself looking at life with utmost indebtedness to many Spiritual Masters, whose help and guidance have been simply invaluable. To look at my accomplishments is to give credit to those who have spent endless hours teaching me the basics of human survival and spiritual knowledge. I cannot tell you of the loving patience rendered to me through my years of learning and contemplation on the higher aspects of the spiritual life. I found that each of us has a childlike seeker festering inside of us who is yearning for spiritual growth. I was a stubborn student, often having to learn the issues of life the hard way, and in many instances a helping hand was there to pick me up off the ground. I remember the first time I sat with a spiritual master of high note in his mud hut sipping a rather unusual tasting tea as he expressed his views of life, existence and the beautiful journey awaiting each Soul as they progressed toward the pure spiritual worlds of God. This experience was the first of many Universal Soul Movement adventures I had "outside the physical body." I still cannot believe how my journey into the true spiritual life began with a book I read in 1975, *In My Soul, I am Free*, by Brad Steiger.

A qualitative change in life can come from the simplest of elements. I have found in my brief span of living in this life that each person is a unit of God's awareness and is seeking to express this to other human beings. It is the nature of human beings to inquire, question, and pursue answers to longstanding situations and emotional crises. What we gather from this world and how we apply it to our quality of living is the standard by which we weigh the merits of the spiritual life. To truly live and endure with dignity is to acknowledge the beauty of all creation as a unified whole. This book has been written with the confirmed reality that each person is searching for new ways to improve his or her life, and is seeking new ways to express their love to others in their personal and impersonal environments. As long as we live, we are tied to a never-ending connection of decisions to be made. It is important to know if our answers fill the empty cup of our inquiries and demands placed upon our plate. *Each question embodies its own answer; after all, this universe is a unity of contradicting forces-in-action.* The purpose of this book is to give the seeker of truth spiritual methods to build individual life strategies for survival in this constantly changing world. As individuals, we must have direction in defining and prioritizing our sacred values and beliefs. Each individual has their own reality and their own way of relating this internal process to others. To test the mettle of what I have mentioned, ask yourself what are the principles and values you believe in, and are you living by those standards? Whatever you know and believe those elements to be, they are not written in stone. This world is in constant flux, and we must move with it to make sense of the world we live in. Our awareness of what we know changes and thus our beliefs and morals change. Beyond the pendulum of negative and positive polarities of existence lies the Pure God Worlds of Beingness that can be individually experienced by the seeker within each of us. Critical views on the entirety of living will change if you, as the seeker, build from your inner sanctum first and your outer world secondly. No one sees the inside of you but yourself, so make the decision to build what you want from this reference point. The outer world is a reflection of the architectural design beginning from this Inner Development. My book offers different rock and mortar to build thy house.

Each of us is born into this life like a child left in a learning laboratory. We must concern ourselves with what materials we feed our minds and souls. Consequently, the teachers we choose to embellish our lives with represent an important as well as critical step in our unfoldment. A mentor of high merit once said to me that good teachers understand they can only help their students to remember what they already know. Thus, the teacher points the way for the true seeker to determine his or her own individual path. This is the process of true spiritual instruction.

*Sri Michael Owens*

# Chapter One

## Karma, Cause and Effect As An Evolutionary Process of Soul

♥ ♥ ♥

*When souls decide how far they will go with the discovery of themselves as souls and an essential part of God, and agree to learn by performing certain assignments per their soul contracts, then those souls begin to understand a new level of their quantum singularity, unfold their wholeness of being, and complete a necessary function in Sugmad's collectivity.*

♥ ♥ ♥

## The nature of karma and how it is related to the concept of "cause and effect"

Karma is the spiritual line of sight, the way and manner Sugmad (also known as God) has chosen to allow souls to recognize their divinity, their eternal natures. Souls' creative actions can set into motion causes that produce effects. Souls can create in the higher realms of their own beingness and bring that energy through to the lowest levels of emotional and physical manifestation. Karma is the mechanism that connects the Inner and Outer Worlds, and helps us to see and understand the immense power of our spiritual natures. Actions begun on the Inner cause energetic ripples that congeal into form, motion and circumstances in our outer lives. Karma affects the interplay of the Light and Sound of Sugmad within our own material creation.

The concept of cause and effect is a simplified way to view the phenomenon of karma for the analytical mind to grasp and use. The more the mind is educated to the ways of the physical and mental worlds through logic and mathematics, the more it runs in grooves that keep it flowing in one direction. Developed Western countries rely more and more on mental processes and perceptions, which limit humankind's ability to see the truth of what is going on at any given time. This is one of countless examples of cultural karma. The cause of holding the logical mind at the top of the hierarchy of truth detectors creates an effect of rigid thinking by blocking out signals from soul, etheric or intuitive, and astral or emotionally based places. This vast, vital energy, which flows continually, and issues forth from God, circulates among the creatures of creation, and does not come from or primarily flow through the Mental Plane to be perceived through the developed mental apparatus of the brain. However, since the leaders of the world are very entrenched in perpetuating logic and mental functions as higher as and better than any other, we of the spiritual hierarchy are now attempting to meet them on their level. If a person has not been able to capture eternal truths any other way, then it is time to understand living truth at a mental level, to start the opening process of all the Inner bodies and faculties inherent in the human body. Simply put, as great teachers have already implanted, cause and effect means you reap what you sow; what you give is what you get.

## How karma relates to past lives

Creations as energy patterns from one life continue the trajectory propelled from the place and time of creation and continue to move out in all directions, but primarily move in the direction created. Death of the material form does not contain or stop the energetic creation and course of action. All thoughts, feelings, and actions contain a measure of power, which cannot be contained in a physical body. Therefore, as souls are singularly responsible for all their acts of creation on any level of their existence, they continue to reap the rewards or consequences of their prior actions, whether remembered or not, until they transmute that energy and all that has been affected by their creation and propulsion into the heart of the Divine Love from which they originally came. Every thought, emotion, and action has an energetic signature, which meets with other souls in harmony or conflict, mutates and continues, either whole or fractured.

Souls, as a piece of Sugmad, are capable of great learning and action, but only so much information and wisdom can penetrate, be absorbed, and be utilized at one time with the mind. Memories of an original event and energetic reverberations felt in the other Inner and physical bodies help souls to learn and integrate the lessons they need, which could not be grasped the first time. Energies take much longer to dissipate - when held in the bodies - than the mind can grasp, especially if a mind is stuck in one pattern and filters out all the rest of the truth emanating in the energy patterns. Immature people do not know how to learn from what happens to them. They get stuck in rigid patterns of belief created from choices made long ago in response to overwhelming situations, which the mind cannot fully comprehend. Instead of integrating energy and information directly as soul without rigid patterns of beliefs about how the world should be, the mind creates facsimiles or memories or karmic patterns that get distorted, as well as rigid. Humans would rather allow these facsimiles of reality guide their actions today than directly perceive a free flowing response to the living moment. This use of distorted facsimiles to guide current action creates a backlog of information needing to be addressed, and creates a bottleneck in the flow of energy into the individual and the collective society. The bottleneck creates increasingly giant reservoirs of energy that becomes harder to deal with and decipher. The mind cannot handle so much information at once; it is too overwhelming, a feeling most abhorrent to human beings, so it either shuts down or chooses an easy and familiar way out, using patterns it already knows and feels comfortable with, even if they are not the best solution. Most minds would rather interpret what is new as facing the unknown and view new information and experiences as threatening; the emotional response is fear, which exacerbates and worsens the response.

If the soul is active, another choice to fear could be excitement and joy at the dawning of a new awareness. Awareness comes from scanning material presented without attachment to what is seen or possible outcomes. As primary guardian of the human body and tool of soul in the lower worlds of duality, the mind is attached to safety, with a perception that what is known is safer than what is not known, and interprets the new and unknown as threatening. The mind is more attached to safety than pleasure, as evidenced by the many ways human beings choose habitual patterns of thought and behavior that consistently lead to pain, rather than risk new choices that would lead to pleasure, often under the guise of propriety or moral law. People would rather continue with addictions, ineffective and faulty communications with self and others, depression, high anxiety, and elevating their egos by not acknowledging the vast amounts of information and experience they have not mastered, instead of humbly admitting the tiny bit they have. Until a person has a breakthrough of some sort and changes his or her beliefs about self and the world and becomes more open to the present moment with fresh sight and heart, he or she will be bound by cause and effect, and continue in ways that keep soul from his or her full awareness and evolution. All of this is designed to show souls many things they cannot learn any other way.

## How the dissolution of negative karma can eventually lead to Self-Realization and God-Realization

One way souls can dissolve karma is by accepting responsibility for all they have created and embrace it all into their true hearts on all levels from whence they came. Like weights removed from helium filled balloons, the dissolution of negative karma frees souls to love and to connect to their Oversouls and the God power with non-power and joy. Freedom results. Love encompasses souls' consciousness with energy and time freed from lower world attachments to pursue increased spiritual discipline. Once negative karma has been resolved, souls are then free to make their own choices about where to go next. The journey is not finished; it has just begun! Souls still need to fully recognize their own power as soul, an eternal spiritual being, without attachment to the physical, astral (emotional), causal (karmic), mental, and etheric (intuitive) bodies they wear to operate in the worlds of duality. Souls are freed from their bonds in stages. The trek to God-Realization is one of the final stages once souls have gained mastery in their lower bodies. Souls must learn to master ever increasing volumes and frequencies of energies, integrate them, and wield them for higher purposes in the ever increasing realms of Sugmad's great tiered heavens that lead to Its fountainhead of joy. There are still many challenges to come, but the love and joy rushing through souls buoy and propel them onward, and with help and guidance from the spiritual masters who have traversed these tricky waters, the upward bound souls can achieve God-Realization and beyond.

## Why soul was placed in a physical universe to unfold and rediscover his or her own eternal nature

Sugmad created souls in order to discover Itself, to realize Its full potential in as many ways as possible. The mechanism for doing so was to place parts of itself as souls into various levels of consciousness, beginning in Its refined state on the plane and vibration where It lives. As part of the way souls could learn more, they were placed in descending coarser levels of consciousness to the densest of all - the physical. Here souls were assigned encasements in clay shells, with multiple levels of illusion all around. In that seed state of forgetfulness, the souls' jobs were to unfold, as rosebuds, into their full natural flower and rediscover their own eternal nature. One cannot fully see what one is and has without experiencing something else. That is why souls were removed from the sublime state of knowingness without form and placed into denser states of form and materiality - in order to play, to appreciate their potential, and explore themselves in relation to other souls with other aims and states of beingness. Like a reed which has been hollowed and poked with holes to make a flute, the breath of Sugmad and souls themselves can then use the reed for more than its original purpose, to express the intention of the breather and bring forth the Eternal Sound in new ways unique to the configuration of the flute and the intention and expertise of the one who wields the instrument. The nature of soul is the breath that ushers forth the sound of love and joy, not the reed or flute, which are necessary instruments of manifestation.

## How soul is an intuitive-reductive unit of God (or Sugmad) and what soul means in this context

Soul is part of God, "made in His image," and is actually the same in nature and structure as Sugmad. Soul is a reduction of the whole, highly sensitive, creative, and giving, or Yang as described in eastern spiritual teachings. Souls also have built into their structures a perfect balance of Yin, or receptivity. The part of this balance used at any given time is a product of the souls' awareness and choices. To rediscover themselves in their full potential, souls must come to know themselves as intuitive-reductive units of Sugmad. The original Big Bang materialized a huge shattering of Sugmad's huge potential of consciousness into countless pieces of souls.

What actually is soul? Souls are a replica of Sugmad, an intuitive-reductive unit of It, parts awaiting their full awakening of life and reunion with their brothers and sisters into their collective mission to know all parts of themselves, in compassionate, detached balance, without judgment or condemnation, in total love and joy. Thus created, each individual soul then began the journey of experience to become more individualized and specialized as choices were made and various experiences were gained in different places and incarnations. Thus, each soul attained singular identification and usefulness to the whole of Sugmad. Consider the human body with its many parts: blood cells, nerves, organs, systems, and more, which grew from the union of a single tiny egg and sperm. Thus the specialization of souls created a vast network of possible combinations of interactions. Naturally, some souls learned to harmonize to work together to build more complex systems; some conflicted and retarded potential growth and demonstration of wholeness. Soul is the atom or the individual unit of consciousness which comprises the Creator and quantum collectivity of Sugmad.

## How Sugmad as a "Universal-Soul" gains reflective experience of Itself through the creative manifestations of soul

As a Universal Soul, Sugmad maintains a position as central executive, ever conveying and renewing Its life energies. With free will given to all souls, Sugmad does not control souls or their destinies. As pure essence with myriad parts scattered in all directions, realms of existences, and levels of consciousness, Sugmad gains reflective experience of Itself through the creative manifestations of souls. Being of the same essence as Sugmad, souls can communicate with, reflect, and tap into this consciousness directly. Sugmad also uses emissaries to assist. Many souls who have gained mastery on various levels of existence serve in silence, in order to guide inexperienced souls. These advanced souls form a spiritual hierarchy to transmit messages back and forth to Sugmad to gain even greater awareness of Its operations and plant seeds for Its desired goals.

Innovative manifestations of souls inspire diversity. Contemplate that. What do you see? There are souls who are sincere, who use humor to express joy, ambitious souls who aspire to interior heights or who are content to solve the mysteries of the Physical Planes, and countless other interests and abilities. No soul can do it all, at least not in one lifetime. Each soul reflects a vast potential of consciousness that contributes to a universal whole.

## Why souls come into this world with a life contract

As every soul is a unique part of the whole, created from Sugmad as part of Its own essence, then charged with much love, energy, and free will on how to utilize its gifts to deal with the challenges of its training, life contracts were created to form agreements between an individual soul and the spiritual hierarchy, including the Grand Council, the Lords of Karma, and the Silent Nine. A life contract specifies a mission; it gives direction as an agreement to move in certain areas to gain awareness and expertise unique to self in relation to others to fulfill a greater purpose. The soul incarnating into the earthly plane has much choice in what it wants to learn and in which direction it wishes to go. In order to keep balance, agreements are needed. In order for soul to understand what it has set in motion, to pay its debts, and reap its rewards according to its choices, life contracts were established.

No two life contracts are identical. As in any large project, division of labor is essential. To build a city, many plumbers and electricians are needed, but there would be nothing if all workers performed the same job. Diggers and removers of dirt, designers and architects of each structure, carpenters, and many more are essential to the completion of the project from start to finish, from the highest office to the most menial of tasks. A life contract is not unlike a job description to focus soul on its chosen tasks, to become accomplished for the good of all life and Sugmad's Best-Laid Plans.

## Why soul must understand its contract, to understand its true purpose in life

Soul must have and maintain a focus in order to make great strides in the confines of one incarnation. Soul's agreements, made with the Lords of Karma before entry into the earthly body, are made voluntarily, in full awareness of what that individual soul needs to learn for his or her benefit and the benefit of all life. The mind as a tool for soul has not generally been able to fully understand soul's true purpose in life, and usually cannot, especially in the lower realms of soul's development. Given the advancement of our earthly civilizations and the degradation of life due to the overpowering dark forces in play, souls now, more than ever, need reminders to stay on track, to understand their purposes and remain on task to carry them out. Especially so for the more mature soul today with a high position in Sugmad's Best-Laid Plans - soul and mind must understand its soul contract.

For example, if a plumber did not understand his job and duties, he might find the mason's job more enjoyable and change course to follow in that direction, abandoning what he agreed to do. Life contracts are more complex and simpler than job contracts and descriptions, and involve various levels of need and operation, but have simple parameters supplying general areas of experience within which to live. For instance, an older soul who has already lived in many positions and levels of awareness and achievement, may contract to develop its spiritual skills and become a leader to help others come to know and follow Sugmad's Best-Laid Plans. Another may come to learn to love. Others are born to "rock the boat" so life stays vital and complacency does not lull souls to sleep. Again, many tasks are needed for the good of all. In each encounter, soul is given greater opportunity and responsibility to carry out his or her mission for his or her own benefit and for the good of all creation and the Creator. Life contracts are a beautiful design and mode of putting forth the kind of agreements that enable souls to utilize their free wills and loving hearts.

## How birth creates a reference point of numerous life conditions

Birth into a physical body provides a place, time, physical family, body definition and limitations, language, social conditions and consciousness, religious expectations, the focus of a nuclear and extended family, and global consciousness. Soul's entry at birth could be smooth or rough; parents or primary caregivers could be loving, abusive, or neglectful. The physical body could be deformed or ill, circumstances could bring disaster or great gifts, each in accordance to the needs and contract of the soul. Each parameter sets a stage for challenges to be addressed in unique soul experiences, is determined prior to entry, and affects the mix. Each soul retains Sugmad's directives, such as free will and retribution for karmic action, and each must follow spiritual laws to move forward in consciousness.

## How soul's contractual understanding of life directly aligns itself with the "discovery of self"

Soul's contractual understanding of life creates and expands its unique viewpoint in its singularity and contribution to the collectivity. When souls decide how far they will go with the discovery of themselves as souls and an essential part of God, and agree to learn by performing certain assignments per their soul contracts, then those souls begin to understand a new level of their quantum singularity, unfold their wholeness of being, and complete a necessary function in Sugmad's collectivity. Souls begin to vibrate and operate in harmony in the quantum collective consciousness, like gears in a gear train. This tremendous expansion of energetic consciousness advances the purpose of Sugmad to live fully and know Itself in Its entirety, under all conditions, in a myriad of possibilities, and increases the likelihood that more souls will regain entry into the God realms in full cognizant awareness. This is how both an individual soul, the collectivity of souls, and Sugmad Itself come to full flower, by discovery of the little and the larger Self. In other words, as souls rediscover their true natures while in the lower worlds of duality, Sugmad learns more about Itself, too. Knowing that agreements were made that limit a person's capabilities or life experiences frees expectations that life should be another way and helps souls focus on the love inherent in their every moment and their return to Sugmad in full consciousness, regardless of their life circumstances.

## Why soul is perceived as a "historical document"

Each soul carries power, wisdom, quest for freedom, and love in a full soul record within his or her expanding energetic signature. Everything that has ever happened to him or her is etched in memory; therefore each soul is an historical document of every life event, relationship, thought, emotion, and action perceived throughout many incarnations. The mind cannot fully identify this information for many reasons, including: 1) Mind cannot follow soul into the soul regions and above the Soul Planes and 2) The mind cannot contain the vast reserves and vast energies that contact with these records would bring. Soul is the knower. Mind is the first tool of action in the lower worlds, after the subtle intuitive sheath connecting the two. Simply, soul perceives; mind performs. Soul is of the pure God essence. Mind is both God and the lower world vibration. Souls contain all they have ever been; therefore, each experience is valuable and adds to the collectivity of wisdom and love - latent and now becoming realized.

## How contemplation opens the door to self-discovery

Contemplation differs from prayer (talking to Sugmad) or meditation (quieting the mind to listen to Sugmad) and works well alone or in conjunction with them. Contemplation is an active form of engaging the mind in activity aligned with soul. It can release souls from their strangleholds and result in Universal Soul Movements. One can contemplate any number of different things, including the Light and Sound of Sugmad, sacred writings, or questions posed to the Inner Masters to free soul to wander the higher realms and reconnect in full awareness with Sugmad. When in true contemplation, the mind relaxes and quiets so that its strong signals do not interfere with the perception of soul on the higher Inner planes. When souls perceive directly, without emotions, thoughts, and beliefs tied to the social consciousness weighing them down, they remember their true origin in the heart of Sugmad and begin their journey home in true and full freedom and love. Know that soul (not mind, emotions, or the physical body) is your true self and awakens your true potential! This is the jewel, the truth, and the key to divine love, freedom and soul's return to the Oneness in full awareness. This accelerates the evolutionary process of the discovery of self!

## A contemplative exercise which will open God seekers hearts to a greater understanding of their lives

1. In a quiet place away from distractions for at least half an hour, relax deeply, let go of all fears and concerns, and then call upon the Inner Master, a beloved spiritual guide, and/or Sugmad for guidance.

2. Imagine a rich, blue veil lifted from your heart and removed from your Third Eye in the center of your head, which awakens all your Inner senses and opens your attention and awareness to a greater understanding of your life.

3. Ask to know your life contract.

4. Sing: "**A LA TU SEN TA**" three times.

5. Listen minutely for the sound of love and joy from the Inner planes; look for the light of wisdom within. Focus on, surrender to, and feel a radiant love pulsing within the center of your beingness.

6. Record any impressions upon your return. Pay attention to clues in your dreams and outer world in the next three days and record those, too. The more you practice and know that the answers you seek will come to you, the more you will gain.

♥ ♥ ♥

# Chapter Two

## The Physical Worlds of God

♥ ♥ ♥

*Soul must break the chains of the physical world's illusions in order to gain a substantial glimpse of the God Worlds, due to the power of illusion to blind soul to its true nature and mission.*

♥ ♥ ♥

## Why the Light and Sound of Sugmad is the foundation of all life, and therefore the mainspring of all religions

Sugmad is the first cause in this universe. All has come from that One Source. Light and Sound are the primary emanations from Sugmad, the frequencies and wavelengths that descend from Sugmad to Earth, which illuminate and amplify energy motion. Light and Sound are the fountainhead of Life and movement from the heights to the depths, an eternal spring that never dies or dries up, always refreshing and rejuvenating. Light and Sound are the Life Force and source of all life and religions.

## Why each plane of existence has a different frequency and calibration of Light and Sound

The finest frequency and calibration of Light and Sound comes from Sugmad, then steps down to coarser frequencies as it tumbles down to each successive plane or level of existence, getting denser and more concrete. This is all part of Sugmad's grand design and mission of grace. From one pole to another, from no form to very dense form, a full spectrum of creation spills forth and befits the magnitude of the Creator. Each plane is distinct to complement creation that came before it and to cause conflict and stimulate motion in every direction so Sugmad can know the full limits of Its range.

## Why soul is in a physical body and develops in a multidimensional universe

We are soul in a physical body and develop in a multidimensional universe in order to know concretely, meticulously, without doubt, that we exist. To know and enjoy corporal reality and the full range of existence, we were sent here to experience our full powers of love, wisdom, and freedom, and to experience fullness versus deprivation, and all other opposition. This is how we come to know ourselves: by comparison. How else can we feel love, without a total lack of love? Soul comes to know itself by its opposition.

## Why Sugmad created the different planes of existence

Frankly, Sugmad created the different planes of existence because being alone becomes boring after a long time. Sugmad wanted to experiment, play, know limits and great capabilities, to understand the battles of the worlds of duality on all levels, to see beyond Itself, and to celebrate life and small gifts after having lost all. There are unique and intensive pleasures on each level of existence. Sugmad wanted to learn and grow and create others to do the same. Sugmad chose to lose and return to love to cherish every moment.

## Why God is called Sugmad in The Way of Truth

Words and sounds carry energetic frequencies, which correspond to different levels of existence and have the capacity to lift soul into those levels. The sound of the word Sugmad (SÜG-MÄD) carries a much higher vibration than the sound of the word God. The word God has been perverted, profaned, misunderstood, and used destructively throughout many hundreds of years. Sugmad carries a sound that is vital and pure on all levels that souls in this universe can traverse.

## Why Sugmad created a unique hierarchy of spiritual administration for each plane of consciousness

Sugmad created a unique hierarchy of spiritual administration for each plane of consciousness for focus and specialization, in order to carry out many unique duties that would become required on each plane of consciousness, and to become grounded in that level of consciousness with increasing expertise. This would be for the same reason salesmen get different training than plumbers or musicians.

## Why Sugmad created a division between the physical worlds and the God Worlds

In the God Worlds, knowledge is universal; it is transmitted and received instantly. Love is ubiquitous, ever present. Souls are Omni-sentient, exuberant, joyful, and free. The God Worlds are a lovely set of planes for souls to explore, but souls cannot experience the full range of awareness and gain the full spectrum of Light and Sound experience within the God Worlds of wholeness. So, the physical worlds were created to provide souls with a greater arena to learn and know more, as a learning laboratory for soul.

## What purposes the Physical, Astral, Causal, Mental and Etheric Plane worlds serve

The Etheric Plane was structured and created to begin soul's descent into the lower worlds, for soul to still be able to intuit Sugmad and the spiritual realms. The mental realm, or mind without physical brain stuff, was made to take the intuitive impulses and step down the vibrations a few notches more. The mental realm also takes input from the lower worlds and can synthesize information to fit with upper Soul Planes. The Causal Plane was created as a storehouse for memory, to be accessible to soul for use in any of the lower worlds. The Astral or emotional plane is the powerhouse for physical movement, a more sensitive transformer of the higher energies than a physical body, manifested so physical vehicles can use the higher energies to continue movement and not slow down and simply die a torturous, laborious death for lack of motion. The Physical Plane was created for souls to experience gross and exquisite corporal beauty and pain from a new sensory apparatus that was developed to operate in this grossest level of being. A full separation was achieved with the crowning glory of the creation of the Physical Plane, the separation of light and dark, ethers or waters of heaven from matter. Now Sugmad's playground was complete and ready for Its grand experiment.

## Why Sugmad delegated the administration and regulation of the physical worlds to Kal Niranjan, Lord of the lower planes

Sugmad delegated the administration and regulation of the physical worlds to Kal Niranjan because Kal has all the required attitudes and attributes for the career: extreme patience, persistence, humor, detachment toward carrying forth distasteful duties, fortitude, strength, willingness, and guile. Kal is not malicious or vicious, as he has been portrayed to be, but he will employ vicious co-workers to do necessary jobs or carry them out himself as required. Kal carries out his assigned duties to Sugmad with precision and deft artistry. He has the stomach for the raw horror that must be carried forth on his watch. This may be strange to read, but Kal can be both a Teddy Bear and a Terror, in equal measure as needed to run his domain. After all, his job is to maintain balance in the lower worlds. He has shown excellence and creativity in the administration and regulation of his assigned domain.

## What role the initiations play in the acquisition and understanding of the level of consciousness on each plane

Initiations are a portal, like a star gate, from one level of consciousness to another. This aspect has been largely unrecognized or appreciated. The Outer initiation is a culmination of a series of tests and Inner ceremonies to acknowledge souls passing of scrupulous training. Initiations provide structure and catapult soul to new uncharted territory on each successive plane as it moves forward through each plane on its conscious return to Sugmad's heart. Each soul is a unique explorer with a unique Soul Contract and trail to blaze. No two souls pursue the exact same course of action.

## What role karma plays in the development of soul

Karma is the Law of Cause and Effect. It states that for every action in the lower worlds, there is a corresponding reaction. It keeps the ball rolling, the gyro spinning, lives in motion, and sets souls on their paths going wherever they have determined to go. Karma creates and sets the course and path for soul to begin its journey. The structure of karma then provides the course to continue. It creates opportunity for soul to take charge, to awaken, to change its own path, to make creative decisions, and to remember what it has encountered and learned. No groove created by lifetimes of repetition is too deep to change; no misery is too great to be lessened. It is not necessary to repeat the past, but it takes creativity, an attribute of Sugmad, and hence soul, to change the easy way or path of least resistance that unconscious souls tend to continue to pursue. Without karma, there would be no momentum or motion and all life would cease to exist.

## Why soul must break the chains of the physical world's illusions in order to gain a substantial glimpse of the God Worlds

Chains of the physical world's existence bind the attention of the incarnated soul to the Physical and Astral Planes by the sheer force and indisputable power of its presence. Soul must break the chains of the physical world's illusions in order to gain a substantial glimpse of the God Worlds, due to the power of illusion to blind soul to its true nature and mission. It takes substantial perseverance and creativity to break free enough to thoroughly utilize the analytical, critical thought processes of the mind. That is why so few souls do so. The Physical Plane, especially when lives are fraught with deprivation, trauma and pain, binds and blinds, and effectively holds soul in its clutches. This is part of Sugmad's design. It may seem unloving to subject souls to eons of pain and loss, but in the bigger picture, it is not so. Once soul glimpses its home in the God Worlds once more, it knows itself as never before, appreciates all life forms and terms of living, and comes anew into its Godhood. Like the useful tool of a pencil, without the sharpening process, soul's growth into full awareness of its Godhood would never happen. To the human body, pain is no illusion; to soul, everything is an illusion and it can change the pain and increase the pleasure of its experience by a mere shift in attention.

## Why each path of life has a Teacher at the helm pointing the way and direction of its spiritual mission

Each Soul must have help, someone to show the way, or it would remain like a squirming animal caught in quicksand, where any movement drags it down. Without hope, inspiration, and glimpses of spiritual succor, people remain lost in their own negative base natures. While the duality of the physical worlds provides rich resources to mine for excellent training, the pull of the negative polarity is far too strong to escape without a teacher at the helm, pointing the way and steering a course free of troubled waters.

## A contemplative exercise to give God seekers facilitated development in the area of their needs in life

1. To determine what you really need at this point in your soul development, get on an imaginary beautiful sailing ship and stand at the helm. It might be like the one that took Peter Pan to Neverland. This ship contains no pirates, only angels, spiritual masters, and other souls like you, all loving and focused on achieving and maintaining Sugmad-Absorption, in order to help others.

2. Ask for what you need.

3. Steer your ship toward the destination you intuit as the course needed in this moment.

4. Take turns with the master at the helm.

5. Open your loving heart as you unfurl the ship's sails and soar high above distant lands and oceans.

6. As you sail the high seas, sing: **"HI DE HU JA VU,"** moderately and repeatedly. Laughter is the wind in your sails.

7. Feel the salty spray with the scent of roses.

8. Notice details.

9. Be sure to write down your experience and the answer to what you need upon your return.

## A contemplative exercise that will give the God seeker a glimpse of the astral, causal, and mental worlds

In the ship and exercise above, you can set your course for each successive plane, from the Physical, upward to Sugmad.

1. Set your dial, with awareness of the Physical Plane set to #1. Feel as fully as you please all sensations you can in your physical body. Sing **"HU NA TRE NA SET."**

2. After you tire of the Physical Plane, set your dial to #2; **place "2" in your middle eye** and feel with astral senses the parameters of the Astral Plane as you leave the Physical Plane behind.

3. Continue to set your dial higher one increment at time, to number three through nine or higher. Continue as long as you can and increase this exploration, shortening the time you spend in the lower realms, as you lose interest in them and desire to explore the higher.

4. You are in control. You can set your dial and set your own course. Do so in alignment with Sugmad and Its open and welcoming loving heart, which is at this minute calling to you, and there is no limit to the heights to which you can travel in full consciousness.

Be diligent and patient with yourself and enjoy!

# Chapter Three

## Metaphysics: The Doorway to Spirituality

♥ ♥ ♥

*In balance, humankind can give voice to the truth of Sugmad and Its creation. In service to heart and Spirit, by focusing on either in turn or both together, souls can learn to experience a fuller range of awareness and aliveness while still manifest in the lower worlds.*

♥ ♥ ♥

## Know your self as soul

Coming to know your self as a simultaneous progression is to begin knowing what is real. What is real, that is, everlasting and permeates all of life, is God, Spirit, and soul. The God power expressed in Spirit and soul gives love, total awareness, and freedom. It is simultaneous, happening all at once, everywhere and progressing according to Best-Laid Plans of the Creator. Sugmad is the core of reality, the basis of reality both in the individual person and in all creation. Coming to know the self as soul, an individual unit of God awareness, is crucial in this time. Soul is manifested in every atom of one's physical body, and every living movement of mind and emotions, and the basis and beginning of karmic/causal reality. It is all connected. All parts are connected by "threads" or units of soul, Spirit, and Sugmad. To know this is to know reality; to not know it is to live in the darkness of ignorance and illusion.

## How service through the heart enhances your spiritual life

The true spiritual path unfolds to seekers through the service of their heart centers and pineal glands because these are the two vital centers of consciousness in the physical body. This is shown to be true by the protective covering of both to preserve life: thick bones of the skull protect the brain; the dense material of the brain protects the pineal gland buried at the brain's center. Many ribs and strong muscles protect the heart. Midway between them lies the throat chakra, to express heart and Spirit. In balance, humankind can give voice to the truth of Sugmad and Its creation. In service to heart and Spirit, by focusing on either in turn or both together, souls can learn to experience a fuller range of awareness and aliveness while still manifest in the lower worlds.

## Why the mental body is sometimes confused with soul

Soul is a unit of God awareness, existing as a piece of a hologram and a resonant chord in a grand symphony of Sugmad. Soul is an integral part, only a part, but a critical part, of the whole. Some theologies confuse the mental body for soul because of the awareness or consciousness that the mental body, or mind, seems to possess. What these theologies or theologians seem to not understand is that all the lower bodies are mechanisms for soul to inhabit and animate. The lower bodies are machines. They are finite, describable, predictable, and can be manipulated by soul. The reverse is not true. There is no life, no movement, and no consciousness without soul. For those who are ignorant of soul, Spirit and God, reality consists of only what can be seen, felt, and deduced from what appears to be only a physical and mental universe. Most of these unfortunates run in circles, maintain a level of confusion, and lack the full awareness of the heart.

## The difference between the mind's knowledge and true spiritual knowledge

Knowledge derived from the mind is limited because it can only perceive that which exists on the level of the mind and below it. It cannot enter, and therefore, cannot perceive anything that exists in the Soul Plane and beyond. Knowledge from the mind loves to "make sense" of things and events, in accordance with physical reality. The mind loves to analyze, synthesize, and categorize, reducing knowledge and life to parts. The mind can be animated and enlivened by soul, but not the reverse. The mind is relative to contingent causal events because that is all it knows and is created to perceive. It has no insight, no foresight, and no hindsight. Such is the realm of soul. Mind and the other planes are dual worlds where opposites continue to vie for attention, tension, and resolution. There is only limited and temporary wholeness, balance, or freedom within these dual realms.

Some philosophers experience problems in making a distinction between mind-knowledge and spiritual knowledge because they do not know any better and have been fed most of their knowledge from preceding philosophers who lacked an awareness of soul. They love mind games and often do not want to admit that there is something beyond them and greater than them, to which they need to become humbled. Ego rules the Mental Plane. Many philosophers love an argument, competition, and to best one another. There is no love for the greater good there, only facts and a quest for supremacy, power, and ego inflation.

## Why the physical world has already been completed

The physical universe as we know it is complete. All there is has been here before, and many times has come and gone. Energy, love, light, and sound cannot be created or destroyed, only changed in outer form. It is the individual's mind that sees with fresh eyes as it shines its attention on one portion of creation after another. This paradox, of course, defies logic of the mind, which relies on physical proof, and so it rejects the concept. All thoughts have been thought; all light has been seen; all sounds have been heard, but not by an individual soul. Untold life forms have existed and created and experienced all that you will in your future. You can ascertain this truth only with the faculties of soul. Sugmad has given everything there is to give. Now it is soul's turn to be creator and continue to manifest the highest glories of the highest Inner realms.

## Why the mind interferes with soul's directions

Soul receives transmissions from God, the Holy Spirit, and other souls all the time. Due to the mind's involvement with its own self-aggrandizement and the running of its physical host and its myriad creations, it tunes out the more subtle whisperings from its spiritual parent, brothers, and sisters, because it deems its work to be of utmost importance. All life forms struggle to survive and the mind is no exception. It prefers its own games and gains to those of soul, which seem less real, tangible and important by comparison. It is only when the mind has achieved all its goals and grown tired of the repetitive nature of life that it will stop its rumblings and machinations long enough to entertain the quiet stillness in which it must rest in order to hear the songs and communications of the spiritual worlds. The mind is an excellent tool, but a poor master. Soul must run the mind for maximum achievement and enjoyment, for the mind cannot even fathom soul, let alone run it. Without soul at the helm, the ship of a person's life will eventually sink or drift endlessly on currents over which it has no control.

## The mind's purpose as a servant to soul

The mind is a wonderful machine that analyzes, munches and crunches information. It is a great storehouse of information and can be utilized in more ways than humankind has thus far ascertained in the current civilization on Earth. With this efficient and useful tool, soul can envision and manifest its own creations, thus proving its godlike powers. Soul is constantly challenged to bring the mind under submission due to the mind's powers to boggle and deceive. It is as if the mind has a mind of its own and soul must be diligent when playing with it because of its deceptive powers. Without the mind, how would soul become separate from Sugmad, recognize its true nature, and find the joy and wonder in discovering itself again? It is no different from sentient life forms having children. The child must be born from oneness, separate to discover its own abilities and uniqueness, and then return to the adult stage with love and respect for the parent who gave it life. This is the cycle of life. Without the mind, there would be no challenge, no fun, and no game.

## How contemplation awakens soul and its relation to daily prayer

Contemplation is the act of soul energizing the mind and then stepping one step further, into itself, beyond concepts and limitations set by the mind. Contemplative exercises practiced daily with regularity will set up a resonance and frequency pattern that awakens souls to their true and eternal natures. In this deeply quiet state of consciousness, souls can experience the Light and Sound of Sugmad and feel great love pouring into their sphere of being. This process will enable the mind to clearly know that there is another, deeper and sweeter aspect to life and to itself. If not threatened with extinction, but given an equal and respected role in the discovery and recovery of its true nature, the mind can be coaxed into service to soul. This is in the interests of the human host and the Best-Laid Plans of Sugmad.

In essence, daily contemplation and daily prayer can be one and the same, depending on the attitude and experience of a person praying. In contemplation, the focus is on the heart center, perhaps the Third Eye, connection to God, opening of the consciousness, and imagining and feeling the freedom and love that results. There is nothing rote about it.

## How life resembles a theatre and we the actors

As master playwright Shakespeare mused, life on Earth is much like a grand theater, and we are like actors on its large and intoxicatingly beautiful and mysterious stage. We each act out our roles, our life contracts, our patterns and habits. At best, the actors grow into fuller consciousness, come to understand the roles they play, and put all their efforts, hearts, and souls into their performances, but do not attempt to direct the whole cast of characters. The director would be Sugmad. Once souls clearly see the parts they are to play, they can settle in and enjoy the skills required to develop themselves as vehicles for their roles and the accomplishments which come from their great efforts.

## A contemplative exercise to develop the practitioner's ability to discern the truth in the words and actions of others

In order to discern truth within one's self and in others' words and actions, one must first let go of emotional turmoil. This is a discipline. One must do whatever it takes to stop viewing through the lens of emotion, for your own emotions will color everything around you. See, own, embrace, and let go of your own anger, sadness, pain, and strife, or you will not be able to discern the greater truth. In order to be aware of oneself as soul, a practitioner must learn to listen to the intuitive whisperings found within the heart center. When soul is awake and connected to another without the clanging of emotions, soul's truth detector will develop quickly, if used rightly and not ignored. To live in reality, attend to your own filters of emotions and beliefs first.

## A contemplative exercise to further develop your ability to discern truth

1. Close your eyes. In contemplation, call upon Sugmad, Dan Rin, and/or a master of great merit, someone with whom you already have a loving connection.

2. Ask to be a loving vehicle for truth and love and to be able to discern truth from non-truth.

3. Imagine connecting heart-to-heart with the spiritual master and Sugmad.

4. Imagine all the love you have flowing out of you into the Great One and then flowing back into your heart with a tender sweetness, a loving light, a gentle music that brings tears of ecstasy.

5. Imagine it and an Inner door will open to it.

6. You may sing **"HU TU SAY HU GAK."** As long as you are within the open heart-to-heart connection, all non-truth will feel and sound hollow, or wrong, like striking a broken bell. This process is done by soul, not the mind. The mind lives in duality and by itself, cannot discern the difference.

## A contemplative exercise to develop a greater communication with soul

1. Visualize a cross section of a nautilus shell. The internal spiral spins on a central axis, which extends straight into your heart.

2. Watch the shell rotate, and draw the structure closer to your body.

3. Feel the rotation and your new ability to move inside it, from one portion or section to another, in and out of center, safe within and free to move.

4. This is your life, your Inner and Outer life and lower bodies. You can stay central and move the shell near or far; you can step inside and slow or increase the spin. You are in control.

5. You are soul and can experience any and all parts of this exercise as you wish. You cannot be harmed, and need not react as you would physically. You can view this experience from any angle you wish. No matter what happens, you chose where you are and what your response will be. You choose. You decide. You align with the rotation or not. You are soul, an integral part of the Great One.

6. You may sing the following mantra aloud or silently: **"TU TE AH SA ALL LA DEMOS."**

# Chapter Four

## The Spiritual Laws of God

♥ ♥ ♥

*We invite all who care to undertake the journey to do so now. Many techniques are being provided through The Way of Truth for eager souls to accept the realities that exist beyond the mundane struggles for existence and the squabbles of ignorant or unloving minds.*

♥ ♥ ♥

## Why universal laws were established and why they supersede all other laws

To bring order into consciousness from chaos, Sugmad established universal laws for all intelligible life forms to adhere to and obey. Sugmad needed a plan and trajectory to get from unformed to formed, from pure love, innocence, and wholeness out into its creations and return home again with all life enriched. Universal laws are like the train track for trains, the Internet for ideas, the heart for loving; without structure, we have no movement or possibility. Universal laws are Sugmad's gifts and vehicles for manifestation.

Spiritual laws come from the highest realms of Sugmad and are true across all levels of consciousness in all space and time. They serve and support the Inner structure of life. Spiritual laws are immutable and are for the benefit of all life. Humanity's laws serve the outer world only. Human laws have become corrupted by human minds and desires that are not in alignment with the highest consciousness; they are subject to the capricious whims and direction of human lawmakers, and are borne and bound by the consciousness that created them. Human laws may be born of love and desire for protection, but do not encompass the majestic span of creation beyond the human consciousness. God's laws serve all life everywhere; human laws serve the group from which they are created.

## How the Law of Love sustains our universe

The Law of Love is the prime directive and life essence of this Sugmad, the Creator of all life in this Universe, all of which is in Its immense sphere. Love is the essential nature of Sugmad, soul, and all manifestation. Love permeates and supports life, transmits life codes, moves, and uplifts, gives joy and pleasure, wholeness and connection. There is nothing without love, only absence and pain. Love is never taken; it is always given. Love can be received, because surrender to love and receptivity to love are the way love is taken in, experienced, and known. As love permeates all of life, the Law of Love shows us that in order to be in alignment with Sugmad and life, in order to get anything good and long-lasting accomplished, we must imbue love in our every waking moment and every action, create and sustain and even destroy with love, for without it, the destruction to ourselves and others perpetuates and grows like a cancer, a black hole, that sucks the life force out, instead of nourishing. Thus, love creates and sustains our universe; the absence of love destroys.

## How the Law of Compassion uplifts our humanity

The Law of Compassion gives souls a way to give love under all circumstances. As souls in life struggle for greater awareness and survival of their manifested forms, they do not have to like all actions they perceive nor all actions taken against their own best interests, whether by themselves or others. However, souls can remain in harmony and in balance with themselves and life if they maintain compassionate, or give neutral love or good will without attachment to the results of whatever is happening. This is the opposite of indifference or hatred, which withdraws love entirely. Souls, through compassion, can remain balanced in their integrity and give freedom to others without being drawn off center and into the drama swirling around them. Love is the essence of life, so Sugmad wants souls to be vehicles for love, to live in and give love to everything at all times. The Law of Compassion gives us the way to do this.

## Why forgiveness and Sugmad's Everlasting Grace are important

Due to the energies of Sugmad and the Light and Sound which pours forth from It into each successive layer and realm, each soul itself is powerful, and souls and their missions are diverse. It is natural and inevitable that souls will conflict, minds will clash, ideologies will diverge, emotions and egos will run rampant, and physical actions will be the effect of all these clashing energies. If forgiveness was not used as a means to surrender what is not understandable or important in the ultimate sense, souls would be unduly burdened and the human consciousness would descend into darkness and chaos. Forgiveness is essential to cleanse the human vehicle, to rid the venom built when the ego's needs are either not met or not perceived to be met. Forgiveness as an act of charity is like sweet smelling soap and a warm shower which cleanses relative reality that does not serve the good of the whole. It is essential for soul to take care of the dual nature of the lower bodies and not allow the ego to hold onto petty hurts or even major traumas. Forgiveness strips away dross and allows soul to flow again in its heart with fluidity, into and out of the heart of Sugmad, and to know first-hand God's Eternal Everlasting Grace toward all life. God's Everlasting Grace is our birthright and our destiny. Let nothing short of Its splendor stand in your way.

## Why the human gift of charity is important

Charity is a gift of love with no strings attached. Charity brings more love to the giver than the receiver. To give is to receive. To give to others with total love, without expectations or thoughts of reward or recognition is the highest form of charity. True acts of charity cleanse the human mind and ego of attachments and vanity and open the heart's spiritual valves for Sugmad's love to flow through unimpeded in greater measure. Since all of life and love is energy (or Light and Sound in essence), gifts of charity, however great or small, allow the essence of Sugmad to flow into even the darkest of places. Souls come to Earth to learn in the greatest arena of all, because when incarnated here, they have all the Inner bodies within reach to easily respond. When souls choose to give freely of their love and kindness to others and make this way of charitable living their own nature, a habit as natural as breathing, souls serve the highest cause. Charitable acts can happen on all levels of beingness, not just physical. In fact, if it does not happen on all levels and only happens physically, as a duty or a "should," it is not charity at all. We are our neighbor's keeper because everything we do affects one another. A smile uplifts and sends a charitable gift of love, without cost, with only benefit to all. Looking for the positive in any given situation, no matter how dark or painful, is a charitable act to all souls, as its energy of love impacts all involved, then ripples into the Inner and Outer Worlds through every soul this love directly touches. Each soul keeps the equilibrium of life in place in some measure. Soul's choices have more impact on others than the mind can ever directly comprehend. Just know this is so. Remember the cliché: "The walls have ears." When humans embrace their baser impulses of greed and anger, and surrender uncaring responses to feelings of love and acts of charity on a moment-to-moment basis, the result is a world transformed. We affect much more than our own lives; we impact the lives of those in our Inner and Outer circles, and the entire collectivity of souls. In this way, we keep the key to open each other's hearts in our own hands. Let us cherish this responsibility and keep the precious key of our loving heart in constant flow through selfless acts of kindness and charity. Better to be a small flame in the darkness than another sun in a cloudless desert sky.

## How using the Law of Silence is a form of love

The Law of Silence is little understood, but greatly needed. It is essential to utilize it properly. Silence is pregnant with power. Silence holds great energetic frequencies of Light and Sound. This is ironic indeed to the western mind, which is used to noise and information overload. This is partly why busy westerners find meditation so difficult and gossip so delicious. It is human nature to share, to give and receive, and to move the tremendous energies inherent after having gathered them from events in a busy day. Some form of venting and distribution of energy is necessary in order to return to balance and maintain equilibrium. One must release these energies responsibly and it is essential to do so to be able to move forward without reaping harsh consequences. One must master the art of becoming adept at holding and channeling these internal, powerful, and often overwhelming amounts of energies. One of the great tests and challenges of aspirants on the spiritual highway home to Sugmad is the aim of learning to work toward the right, discriminate use of these energies and silence. Sugmad and the Inner Masters will often train souls in use of this little known, but vital Law of Silence. Souls often fail as they learn their lessons, and thus earn their just rewards, but souls will be tested time and again. The Silent Nine wield tremendous power and authority due to their mastery of this art.

Using the Law of Silence properly is a high form of love. As each soul is in a unique position in the vast arena of soul development, each soul receives the challenges needed to move forward, learn and grow in wisdom, love, and freedom. Souls are trained on the Inner planes, and as they understand and can tolerate knowing and changing long held views connected to their karma and the social consciousness, truths of varying degrees and power will be revealed. Soul's lessons come in forms not previously acceptable to the mind, but which the mind now desires and begins to examine and use for soul's further mastery. The lessons gained on the Inner states of consciousness are often for that soul alone and not to be shared for various reasons. One reason is that sharing secret teachings would dissipate the power inherently held by keeping silent, which would spoil the lesson and ruin the abilities of the aspiring soul to move into greater levels of mastery. Secondly, information shared by the Inner teachings is often suitable only to the soul who perceives it and not for others in that person's life, possibly not even their mate. Information that helps one soul may hurt another who is not yet ready to learn it or who has already learned the lesson and moved on. Much discrimination must be used when receiving the secret teachings. Inner lessons are an energetic consciousness needed to gain wisdom, power, detachment with compassion, and freedom. Wisdom and insights gained may cause conflict and imbalance in a soul for whom the lesson was not directed. Sharing these gifts with those for whom the teachings were not meant might cause arguments and derail soul's progress on one or more levels. Souls must learn caution and right discrimination in wielding power. It is essential for all souls desiring to rise higher in consciousness and serve Sugmad's Best-Laid Plans to learn the proper use of the Law of Silence. Such service is the highest form of love. Love is the breath of life and silence is a gift of holding and giving love.

## How the Law of Freedom relates to free will

The Law of Freedom illustrates that Sugmad has granted all souls free will: freedom to explore all the worlds, to learn and grow, to make choices, to move into any area desired and create whatever souls want. Freedom creates, contains, and maintains the vital energy of life. This great gift has the potential to set souls free to soar into the God worlds and straight into the heart of Sugmad, to return as co-workers and distributors of God's love, if they so choose. The Law of Freedom enables Sugmad to learn of Its true and full potential. On the negative side, freedom has certainly caused great misery, as immature souls have misused their power. Spiritual law grants freedom. Human law restricts freedom, purportedly in the best interests of managing the collectivity. Certainly some human laws propel souls and society forward, toward the best for all with minimal pain. Many will point to the Ten Commandments as basic spiritual guidelines for healthy living. Sugmad and Its assigned representatives have long guided humankind, because souls are so creative and impressionable; they can easily be swayed into thoughts and actions that bring immediate pleasure without thought of consequences.

However, Sugmad has a bigger plan than a perpetual smoothly running collective consciousness. Sugmad's plan involves souls gaining immense freedom, love, wisdom, and power, in order for each soul and Sugmad to know itself in Its entirety. This goal only happens with soul's freedom to make a wide range of choices and fail in small ways in order to succeed on a grander scale. It is better to lose a battle and win the war than the other way around. Freedom is life enhancing. Restrictions of freedom may give temporary stability and peace, but the cost is far too high in the grand scheme of life. Safety can restrict growth. Sugmad is about growth, not safety. Sugmad and soul are eternal, so safety is not a prime concern. The human consciousness and body are both finite and subject to pain and death. Soul learns by doing, not by not doing. Human laws and social restrictions doubly bind soul by cutting off areas of exploration, confining vision, and reducing expectations and potentialities. How can one learn responsibility without any? Free will is central to the Law of Freedom. As all souls are granted free will to act, they expand within the spectrum of development in their long tenure on Earth and in the Inner realms. As a soul breaks through layers of boundaries, it realizes that it is God; it becomes God-Realized and eventually God-Absorbed, voluntarily giving all it has to the cause of the whole. Only with a prime directive of freedom can a chicken break out of an egg, grow to adulthood, produce more eggs, and continue the cycle of life.

## How the use of the Law of Noninterference renders respect to all life

Since all souls are granted freedom by Sugmad to grow in their own unique ways, the Law of Noninterference is needed to define the responsibilities souls have to one another and to God to not limit their innate freedom. The Law of Noninterference reminds us to give freedom to all, to not interfere with another person's choices, for doing so interferes with the realm of creative possibilities and Sugmad's will. This does not mean we allow everyone to do anything harmful that they want. We still have the freedom to protect our lives, our personal and collective boundaries, our thoughts, and our individual freedoms. There are many ways to accomplish certain goals. Creativity may be called for to reduce the tendency toward grosser forms of force. If they remember the Law of Noninterference, souls can utilize conflicts of interests to produce new solutions, using the energies and wisdom of joining opposing forces, increasing finesse, detachment to outcomes, refinement of thoughts and actions and more -- to advance mutual understanding, create win-win situations, and grant more freedoms. The Law of Noninterference applies to children as well, but great discernment is required in this area. Noninterference does not mean we allow children complete freedom, especially in life threatening situations, for they typically have less wisdom and more impulses for immediate gratification. Children's caregivers must act responsibly and guide them, as is their duty and responsibility; this often involves some intervention and restriction. When children are immature, they need structure to test their strengths and learn. They also need much freedom to grow to increase their awareness and skill levels. Without freedom, children will wither and die an interior death, if not physically. The Law of Noninterference renders respect for all individuals and all walks of life. No race, country, creed, ideology or spiritual path is better than another; each has its place and time that are beneficial for some souls. Diversity is essential. Immaturity, even with its distasteful by-products, contributes to the grand scheme of life, even if only to show what damages and destroys. Human beings loathe destruction and chaos, but those aspects of life are also vital and are necessary components to maintain balance in the worlds of duality or manifestation. The Law of Noninterference reminds us to respect others and ourselves, or be diminished and reap further consequences of such choices.

## The Law of Unity and how it relates to "Universal Oneness"

The Law of Unity reminds us that our true goal and state is union with Sugmad and with one another. In this state of Universal Oneness, we do not loose our individuality, our unique experiences, capabilities, or awareness. Instead, we join forces with the collective energies that propel us from a single unit of awareness into a quantum universality of collectivity. When exercising freedoms may initially separate souls, the Law of Unity reminds us of our return to this glorious union, to join our separateness into a greater awareness and a unifying whole. Soul is innately geared toward this goal, and may seek to achieve it in a myriad of ways, some which may produce the opposite result of separation and despair. The mind cannot fully grasp the message from this page, but soul can experience and know the truth, majesty, and wonder of this union. The purpose of Sugmad is the activation of full consciousness. Some people may think that Universal Oneness means sameness, mediocrity, limitations, or even a state of perpetual peace. This is not so. The activation of combined polarities produces an energetic explosion that would be the opposite of all that the mind holds dear. We are just beginning to experience the potentiality of this Law of Unity, as many souls have achieved spiritual mastery and are returning to Sugmad with pure and selfless hearts to move the collectivity forward. The successes of the few open a door for many others in the next wave of migration back to the Heart of Sugmad.

## How contemplative prayer connects the participant with the Word of God

Contemplative prayer provides a way for the mind to engage in the machinations of Soul. The mind is such a powerful and useful tool, which can be employed to perceive some of the Inner teachings and lessons of soul in relation to its many aspects. The mind must be trained to focus on the highest spiritual realms and principles in order to engage the emotions and physical body to act in accordance with the highest will of Sugmad. The mind has great capacity, but if the culture in which it has been raised is negatively focused on materiality, the mind will return to the habits and beliefs with which it is accustomed. Hence, soul always longs to return to Sugmad's loving embrace, but the mind finds stability and comfort in social constructs and conventions, as well as its own importance within those spheres. This conflict can be resolved through a daily practice of contemplative prayer. Humble, conscious, thoughtful communication with Sugmad and Its spiritual messengers can bring into alignment the lower bodies in service to soul. Through sitting still, with outer senses withdrawn from the outer distractions and free to perceive the subtle nuances of the Inner worlds, the mind can begin to understand the power, love, glory, and freedom that it can enjoy when aligned with soul and its mission on Earth. Through focused alignment with the Light and Sound, the practitioner of contemplative prayer can open to, receive, and hear the Word of God. Success takes training and receptivity, willingness and surrender, to relax and project into the higher frequencies of the God realms. We invite all who care to undertake the journey to do so now. Many techniques are being provided through The Way of Truth for eager souls to accept the realities that exist beyond the mundane struggles for existence and the squabbles of ignorant or unloving minds.

## A contemplative technique to develop more love and compassion for others

Surrender, humility, and unfettered love are foundational to the development of more love and compassion for others.

1. Sing **HU** six times, with gratitude and an open heart full of love.

2. Surrender to a feeling of increasing joy flowing from the heart of Sugmad to your own heart. Humbly know you are but a servant to life, one who may ask for what you want and receive the blessings that help in Sugmad's will and ways.

3. Ask the Inner Masters to guide you to develop more love and compassion for others.

4. Sing: **"HU RAY TA MAIN."**

5. Visualize great waves of HU.

6. Listen to the Great Current of Sound that can fill your Inner and Outer ears with song.

7. Imagine and feel Sugmad's love wash through your heart, mind, and all bodies, gently, as a warm shower or gentle rain, increasing your purity of love and focus on the Light and Sound vibrations as it moves through you.

8. See all impurities still inside any of your bodies, including emotions or thoughts of a social nature, flow out through your feet into the Earth, which can absorb and transmute all negativity into its fiery core without a shred of disruption to its mission. Let go!

Practice this cleansing daily, until you can visit and swim joyously in the great Sea of Love and Mercy that comprises Sugmad's heart. Remain open to Sugmad's subtle whispers in every moment of your day or dreams, especially from others in your life, with gratitude and surrender.

## A contemplative technique with a mantra that will develop a deeper use of the participant's skills to resolve personal problems

1. Sing **HU** six times, with gratitude and an open heart full of love.

2. See, hear, and feel joy flow from the Heart of Sugmad to your own heart and out into the room or location where you are and then out into the world.

3. See, hear, and feel soul dancing lightly and joyfully on these expanding, colorful, harmonious waves of love, simultaneously out into the world and deeper into the Inner Worlds into the higher

realms. Soul's focus may be larger than the universe or smaller than an atom. As soul, there are no limits to where you may place your attention and receive knowledge and wisdom. All the Inner and Outer Worlds are connected. Be the bridge; be the connection.

4. Ask Sugmad and one of the Masters to guide you to develop a deeper use of your skills to resolve your personal problems.

5. Sing: "**TU SAY TRE TU SAH, TU SAY TRE TU SAH MAY.**" Obstacles will begin to dissolve on all levels in direct proportion with your measure of purity of love and focus of attention of utilizing the Light and Sound energies toward your mission. Pay close attention and trust that whatever you experience is in accordance with your state of consciousness. Loving devotion to Sugmad's Best-Laid Plans will raise your level and states of consciousness. Listen closely and make it so.

♥ ♥ ♥

# Chapter Five

## The Spiritual Streams of Reality

♥ ♥ ♥

*As the consciousness becomes refined and experiences of a finer nature awaken soul's faculties of perception, soul begins to know itself as distinct from its accoutrements, the robes or sheaths it uses to perceive various levels within God's multileveled kingdom and begins to awaken to its true nature and the nature of the greater realities beyond itself.*

♥ ♥ ♥

## Why the meaning and nature of reality is an important subject to address

Reality exists on a multitude of levels, far beyond the physical realm that eyes can see and mind can comprehend. The social consciousness knows but a small slice of reality. Religions point to a greater reality, but cannot fully explain it. Reality is what exists, in form or potentiality. Its subtle essence and potential extend from the grossest levels of creation to finer psychic levels to the spiritual realms and into the Ocean of Sugmad and beyond. It is important to know of reality's multiple facets, so that souls can begin to know their true nature and potential and take steps to reach beyond their preconceived limits, grasp the core of truth, and then manifest their dreams, not only for themselves, but for the collective good.

## How true surrender to Sugmad's Will carries the God seeker into the pure God Worlds

Surrender to Sugmad's will takes the God seeker into the Inner realms of pure love and Light and Sound, far beyond the mundane physical reality of the common man. Surrender to Sugmad's will means letting go of the mental apparatus and modus operandi, going beyond the needs and desires of the individual ego, and moving beyond the teachings of the greatest philosophers, prophets, saviors, and savants. True surrender is a mainline into the very Heart and Soul of Sugmad, a linking of a part to the whole, like a cell is linked to a human.

## Why understanding physical reality is necessary to understand spiritual reality

Physical reality is a springboard for understanding spiritual reality due to its coarse and obvious nature. No soul living on Earth can deny what the majority can clearly see, hear, taste, smell, and feel. Maturity provides awareness that perceptions of physical realities can vary according to the individual. Due to the evolution of thought and language, incarnated souls can discuss, identify, and create subtle realities, and can share in abstractions, which only some of their kind can understand. As the consciousness becomes refined and experiences of a finer nature awaken soul's faculties of perception, soul begins to know itself as distinct from its accoutrements, the robes or sheaths it uses to perceive various levels within God's multileveled kingdom and begins to awaken to its true nature and the nature of the greater realities beyond itself.

## Why events in the physical world are reflections of the "higher" spiritual worlds

Sugmad is the first cause. Sugmad creates souls in the realms of pure consciousness, without form, with only Sound and then Light. At one time, these high spiritual waters were all that existed, until coarser levels sprang forth, first by the will and thoughts of Sugmad and then by the will and thoughts of individual souls and groups of like-minded souls. All manifested life and forms spring from higher spiritual waters, the pure Inner planes, down through the dual planes and into the physical. Variance, more interesting and challenging, begins when one splits into two, and then continues to divide and differentiate. As souls in the Inner Worlds separate and clash, their vibrations go forth, manifesting outwardly into grosser material form. Thus charged, conflict may perpetuate along predetermined lines of trajectory, engaging more souls of similar vibration. Since Sugmad created each soul with a unique signature, purpose and vibration, countless lines of motion and emotion pour forth, some harmonizing, some cacophonous, some expanding, some contracting, some creating, some destroying. Minor skirmishes may evolve over time and intensify into major partitions, battles, and even war. Each soul's individual environment is a compilation of individual responses and choices, made over eons of time; in other words, soul's karma is born and carried aloft on its movement through Light and Sound and time and space, and intensifies in the absence of love.

## Why it is necessary for soul to take a physical shell

Souls were placed in physical shells to break down the chains of reality to know themselves in all forms, in all ways, in all variations of themselves, to come from wholeness into separateness into waves of change, into a multitude of variations to learn to love not only themselves, but also all life in totality. To love is to mend the brokenness, to return from bondage to freedom, with responsibility and caring for more than just one's self, to love and listen without separation.

## Why the illusions of the lower worlds are necessary for soul

Soul generally learns though direct experience with a thing itself, its values and purposes, and by its opposite. How well does soul know love except by the absence of love, light without darkness, cold without heat, hardness without softness, male without female, and life without death? Souls learn more fully of their own essence as creators and children of Sugmad by illusions that strip them of their true glory - beings created of and surrounded by immense love, even the presence of Sugmad. Part of the grand illusion is that souls are separated, rejected, or lost. This is how souls move through the universes and gain wisdom, freedom, and joy. Does this seem paradoxical to you? Remember that although the human embodiment of soul incorporates the mental, causal, and emotional bodies, these are not the realms of Sugmad, nor the home of Sugmad, but the tools

Sugmad uses for training souls to fully know their capacities and have them return willingly from their experiences in every direction with full surrender to Its greater ways and love and service to Its lesser ways. Without illusion, souls would not take their lessons seriously, would not focus, would not create, would become complacent and nonproductive, and the lower worlds with all its life forms would cease to exist. The game of life would cease, along with its rich experiences. Illusion is only painful when souls deem it so.

## How fear blocks the true reality of Sugmad

Fear is the antithesis of love. It is a watchdog of the Astral (emotional) Plane, a mechanism set in place for survival of the physical body to protect that body from physical harm. Fear's face is ever turned toward darkness and reflects the dark side in all its attributes. A clear vision of reality comes when soul faces the Light and Sound of God in the totally opposite direction. Fear alerts; love awakens. One cannot have fear and a clear vision at the same time.

## How the highest use of "non-power" reveals true reality

The non-power is the royal highway to Sugmad's very heart. Its central beacon spotlights the core aspect and attribute of soul's pathway from the chaos created in the lower worlds into the heart of love. The non-power connects hearts and pulses with energetic frequencies, which are pervasive and whole. When soul's incarnated outer bodies align in non-power, they are jolted awake and cleaned and cleared of the debris which clouded soul's vision; only then can the meaning and purpose of life become crystal clear. Non-power is the receiver, the receptacle of the Sugmad Power. To be in the core of who we are, at the center of our power where Sugmad plays us like a flute, we must remain neutral amidst the surging of opposing forces and remain in the non-power of the greatest Power. This is true detachment with full love and awareness. To know the truth of this, one must experience it.

## How the ego perpetuates illusions

The ego is confined to the lower body reality and aligns with the personality of the mind and protective mechanisms in the emotional and physical bodies. Ego's purpose is survival. Too often ego is seduced by power. It does not discriminate between love and power and so must be balanced by soul to maintain a vision of non-power. Since reality is vast and far beyond the ego's ken, and encompasses all Inner and Outer states and realms, ego cannot see and know the vast worlds beyond. For a visual representation, compare ego as a ping-pong ball to the Sun.

## How "beliefs" and "faith" form present and future realities

Belief is a mental function, a solidified thought form sometimes confined to an individual, but more often held by a collective consciousness. Faith is an action one takes to rely with total trust in a belief or set of beliefs. As thoughts form and build one upon another, beliefs arise and steer the course of an incarnated soul by guiding present and future actions. These become the lenses through which a person views reality. Hence, once perceived realities are set in motion, a tremendous force is usually needed to change course, thus practically insuring a certain route and destination. So, the future of societies and religions become predictable based on a series of choices made and built upon fixed beliefs.

## Why positive memories should be retained and others disregarded

The mind loves habit. Beliefs create the realities that bind souls' actions. Therefore, the God seeker must choose to build upon positive memories Spirit has given, instead of holding onto rigid beliefs that lead to misery or staying stuck, in order to keep moving forward toward achieving and maintaining unconditional love, objectivity, neutrality, serenity, and surrender to Spirit's gentle whisperings. Since life in the physical world is vital and changing, beliefs can easily become outdated and hold soul in a pattern that is no longer true or constructive to its movement toward Sugmad. Barring a firm foundation and trajectory toward Sugmad, memories that arise as thoughts and feelings can captivate the mind, hold it in negativity, and perpetuate destructive patterns. Focus and build upon positive memories from Spirit, instead of indulging in the negative results of events, or worse, on the sensationalism of modern media. This choice will bring happiness, because it is one's attention and awareness that will continue to forge a strong path in any direction that soul and mind chooses. Disregard anything that is not from the Light and Sound of Spirit, for all else is illusion, and leads in a spiral downward. Objectivity facilitates the awareness of truth.

## A spiritual exercise to help God seekers set daily priorities

Start and end your day for the next week with the following: With an open loving heart and willing attitude, say the following as a reverent prayer/mantra:

> *"Show me thy ways, Sugmad. Lead and guide me to the best path for me to take in each moment today. Please help me set my priorities to best serve*

> *your will and bring me what I most want and need, for the good of all the people in my life, including me. I willingly and gratefully open my Inner and Outer eyes, ears, and heart to learn from my internal and external reality as it truly is, and not just as I perceive it. Allow me to maintain balance and objectivity as I grow to understand what it is you would like me to do."*

Be sure to record the intuitive wisdom that will begin to be revealed and build upon it. Spirit and spiritual masters will make their presence and wisdom apparent. Capture what you receive, because no matter how real and strong your experiences will be, they can easily be lost. Build on the positive memories Spirit gives you and disregard the rest with objectivity.

## A spiritual exercise to help God seekers attain true reality now

At any time throughout the day, sing "**HU SA VA**" three times and say, "I can create anything I want. I create love and peace in my heart in every moment, joy and fulfillment no matter what I do, wherever I am or whoever I am with. Please reveal truth and help me perceive accurately."

Focus on Sugmad is what counts and gives the energetic confirmation needed to align with the highest laws and intent of the Great One.

♥ ♥ ♥

# *Chapter Six*

## *Of Things to Come*

♥ ♥ ♥

*Changes will not come as you imagine. Your consciousness is the only asset you own.*

♥ ♥ ♥

## Why it is important to keep informed of today's times regarding religion, political changes, and advances in the scientific and medical communities

Too many times people are told to only take responsibility for their children, family, self, and immediate community. Some teachers say to only take care of self, get to Sugmad alone, and then give only love. In the past, that may have been all that was required, but today, we are a global family and a global village as never before. The needs and consequences of one soul rapidly become that of the next soul - across the world. Weaponry and savagery are increasing and strangling all of life. A responsible soul learns from whatever is available and takes action to halt humanity's self-destruction. Each soul has been given the privilege and responsibility to co-create this world, with Sugmad and with one another. Each soul can contribute so much to balance in the world, if not in physical action, then at least by working inside themselves with their consciousness. Why let a few loud fanatics corral and force the rest of the silent, responsible, loving majority into acts of barbarism, limitation, disease, and misery? It is up to the brave and loving and the bold and adventurous to step up and make advances for all humanity to insure Earth's survival and the evolution of all life. Those who do this are heroes of the modern age, whether their acts are done in full view of the media or in the silence of their hearts. The world is such a tormented and precarious place now; it is incumbent upon all souls to draw upon their greater resources to advance life into health and harmony or perish. Are you a puppet, victim, or co-creator of all that you want to see manifested upon this planet?

Each person's personal dream reflects and affects the universal consciousness. As all souls connect in the subterranean subconscious river of Spirit, knowing that the manifestations of others affect the global community can be instrumental in making personal and global adjustments in consciousness for the good of the whole. As each soul as a universal citizen learns what his brothers and sisters have created and steps out of his or her own little world long enough to take into his or her heart and soul the essence of the direction of the planetary consciousness as a whole, s/he can take some silent and conscious breaths to reassess personal beingness in the grand scheme and use what has already been manifested to further the personal dream and the collective dream toward any aspect of the positive end s/he seeks. Souls are joined as one and can draw on the universal energy as one if souls stay out of negative destructive energies and continue to perpetuate the vision of their true hearts. Simply put, we each can step into the river of life as it flows and manifest our dreams in the same positive direction. We can use the flow already established to steer away from what is not helpful and welcome in what is. We can use what is to create what is not. Together we can manifest a glorious future that has never happened before, or we can continue to repeat the petty mistakes of our predecessors and perpetuate self-destruction on a massive scale. Knowledge is power on the Earth plane. Wisdom gained from the experiences of others, as well as your own self, can guide executive decision-making.

## How this planet is continually protected from self-destruction by the intervention of the Archangelic hierarchies and spiritual masters commissioned by Sugmad

Throughout the last several million years, the Earth has been protected from destruction by cosmic forces, solar flares, internal cataclysms, humanity's errors in thinking, and individual and collective rash emotional and egotistical perturbations. Compared to the vastness of space, there are few places in the Physical Plane amenable to sentient life forms through which souls can enter and grow. In many ways, Earth has been lovingly protected, nurtured, and guided as a model planet in its development of consciousness by Archangelic hierarchies and spiritual masters commissioned by Sugmad. Inspired thoughts and visions in explorers, warriors, artists, musicians, government officials, business leaders, and the common people have moved consciousness forward in creation and in loving Sugmad, self, and others. A few avatars in every age became popular; many more remained sequestered and schooled a few ready and willing souls to do the arduous work required to advance into high spiritual realms and return in service to the whole. Life might have evolved without the protection of the spiritual hierarchy, but what a “crap shoot” it would’ve been!

Knowing that the Archangelic hierarchies and spiritual masters have been commissioned by God to guide and protect the Earth and all its inhabitants can help a soul to remember to call upon them for assistance and to consciously align with them in spiritual times taken throughout the day. One can consciously commit to being part of a plan far greater than any personal vision. This knowledge alone can bring hope where focus on emotional or physical failures has brought only despair. Many souls get caught in the illusion that the Inner realities must be seen and heard as loud and clear as physical reality; but this is not how it is. The spiritual hierarchy moves in silence, although many times they bring the sound current, which can be heard by many who listen with the heart and Inner ears. As Earth’s planetary consciousness begins to open again to the presence of the Holy Spirit and its many carriers on the Inner and Outer arenas of life, much time hardened dogma created in the wake of previous spiritual giants and saviors of long ago may loosen and fall of its own heavy and often corrupted weight. Focus on light and love; darkness will naturally disappear. Focus on music within silence and joy will appear. Help has always been available, but has never been as strongly needed and available as it is today.

## How the Internet, computers, media and scientific advances are being channeled and directed by intelligent life forms from other planets

All souls have free will and are created from the creative energies of Sugmad through Its spiritual essence. All souls are hence interconnected and can reach out for quests to satisfy a longing in any area of their choosing. When creative technical minds set out to solve a series of problems to manifest what has not happened on Earth before, their call of soul goes out through the vast Inner network of spiritual connectivity. Once intelligent life forms on other planets realize that souls require information, they reach out to connect. What greater joy is there than teaching another soul who is eager to learn what you have spent so much time learning and developing? How many times have people developed their unique area of expertise, only to be frustrated that so few around them, especially those closest in their family, could care less about their life's love and endeavors? It is no different in many other worlds. Each soul gets to choose its own direction within an infinite arena of possibilities and the mandate of free will. Once sentient beings awaken to their true nature as soul through their efforts and the guidance of the spiritual hierarchy, they too can learn to reach out for the connection needed to pass along valuable information, which will help their fellow souls advance along the spiritual and physical life continuum. Space and time are not barriers to soul's universal movement and communication. This interconnectivity has happened long ago and is happening now.

Once visions and systems come into manifestation, more minds are sparked by possibility; then God's wish of full development expands exponentially as souls find their calling, fulfill their life contracts, and move in the direction of collaboration for the greater good. Beings from other planets have developed many technologies that have helped them and can help citizens of Earth. Some civilizations in other worlds have not been as emotionally engaged as human beings have been, and so have been able to put their vast creative energies into technologies that save lives and uplift consciousness. Humans have been fighting too long, pitting egos and ideologies, and trying to press their own visions of reality on one another rather than grant others the freedom of thought and beingness that the Creator has given to all. Once hearts and minds open to the full range of possibilities and apply them constructively to all life without the greedy desire for personal gain that has so hindered the western mind, there is no limit to what can be accomplished.

## How other life forms perceive humanity's present state of consciousness

As individuals within a collective structure, other life forms perceive humanity's present state of consciousness in many ways. Great excitement prevails as the collective consciousness of Earth moves forward into greater maturity and understanding of that which has previously been kept secret by the leaders who knew, but were crucified or murdered for telling. The proliferation of information and availability of reception in an ever-increasing number of homes is causing humanity to awaken to levels of consciousness previously unknown. That these multitudes collide, especially in the area of old traditions versus new is totally understandable; conflict naturally arises. Conflict, collision, and resolution have happened everywhere, in all life forms, as progress changes the "natural order" and life grows out of its previous shell. Other life forms who watch the events transpiring in the public sphere on Earth are fascinated at the similarities and differences to their own history. Many merely watch amused; many offer their expertise to assist. Due to the contingencies of free will, souls on Earth must reach out to them, hence, The Way of Truth's emphasis on learning Universal Soul Movement within the constraints of unconditional love, compassionate detachment, and balanced responsibility. The groundwork has been laid. Many "wild cards" have thrown monkey wrenches into the engine of life, but the mechanics in place serve the greater cause and cycle of life's expansion, its movement out in all directions, its return to Sugmad in love, and its outward movement again. Souls who see the whole picture are delighted. There is little skepticism and great desire to help remove certain societal concerns and long standing karmic engrams to keep moving forward with Sugmad and life's plan.

## Why other life forms feel it is not against the free will of Earth's inhabitants to interfere with the normal affairs of this planet

Humanity cannot solve its problems by being in the same state of consciousness which created the problem in the first place. Souls must move to higher states to solve the problem. Some life forms who think too much and know nothing of the big picture think they should never interfere. However, to balance the energetic frequencies of the universes and move forward with Sugmad's Best-Laid Plans, humanity needs interventions from higher consciousness. Many inhabitants of Earth cry out for help. What happens on Earth affects souls that inhabit and move through all the various planes and frequencies and can wreck havoc with their homes or help elevate souls in their worlds. All are interconnected! Interventions are the way humans have long helped one another on Earth; when people are in crisis, those who thrive on the art of rescue rush in to help, whether in physical, emotional, or mental areas or in private or public sectors. Every migration of human life from one area to another has been predicated on exploration for the love and adventure of discovery. When one part of an organism becomes sick, it is the nature of life to fix any problem that threatens its life and comfort. Survival is primary.

## How mankind utilizes each spiritual body (astral, causal, mental, etheric, and soul) in a shape and manner that has attracted the attention of other life forms

On Earth, humans in various cultures developed different coping mechanisms, illnesses, psychological responses, and modes of thinking and behavior. The human form creates similar internal responses across cultures, climates, world events, and other influences that shape human norms and outer activities. Sentient life forms elsewhere can be very different, and so are intrigued by human decision-making. The human form is relatively vulnerable and fragile and has developed many strategies to adapt to its environment over its evolutionary process. Astral bodies need love to survive, anger to prompt protection, sadness to awaken to self-destructive tendencies, and other emotions as an alarm to awaken protective responses. The causal body responds to the other bodies and holds its secrets for further exploration and building, although few humans seem to use it well for its intended purpose. The human mental body and its systems have produced an astonishing array of beliefs and disciplines. Humans, developed in response to survival, are exceptionally creative and responsive, but life does not respond to need alone. Life responds exponentially to creative expression and love for the good of the whole. Some souls are moving their creative energies across the physical and interior universes with love, detachment and freedom to respond to the cries of the destitute. Since everyone needs upliftment and unfoldment, soul truly longs to uplift and help others, not bring them down. Souls on Earth have developed a history of acting from the heart, helping the “underdog” when times get tough, and have learned to fill themselves and others with joy. Of course, the opposite is true for many souls too. This creates hugely positive life changes that can be applied in any universe. Pioneering souls are learning to stretch beyond the illusion of lack to the infinite realm of potential through their intuitive sheath that connects the mind with soul. Humanity is moving out of its adolescence in many areas. The Way of Truth brings a collaboration of a myriad of teachers to provide eager souls with gifts not previously seen on Earth or on other planets. At this juncture of environmental and military crises in which Earth inhabitants find themselves, much can happen in any direction. The stage is cast; players have rehearsed and are well prepared to act. Many are anxious to utilize their destructive tools to incorporate their distorted thoughts and beliefs in Earth’s inhabitants. Earth’s mysterious future hangs in the balance.

## Why other life forms exhibit a different frequency of Light and Sound in their spiritual bodies than human beings

Other life forms exhibit different frequencies of Light and Sound in their spiritual bodies than human beings as part of Sugmad’s playful experimentation with creation. There can be no limit or end to Sugmad’s grand and interconnected design. A multitude of life forms beyond the mind’s comprehension have been and will continue to be created to respond to God’s directive to know Itself and respond to Its great and never ceasing love under an infinite number of conditions. Relatively few souls have been gifted with a physical body. The Physical Plane is the place for souls to experience all levels at the same time -- the full and complete range of experience. It may not seem to be this way to many who suffer from the painful illusions to which soul is subject in its infancy, but souls who come into the Physical Plane on Earth and other planets are special in their ability and gifts of life in this plane, where soul can learn valuable lessons and receive life's wondrous bounty.

Each life form corresponds to its respective environments for survival first, then self-actualization, and then God-Realization and God-Absorption in all essential levels of energetic beingness. Sugmad does not act according to the human approach to perceiving and making sense of the worlds; Sugmad does not act as the human penchant for a "cookie cutter," "one size fits all", only one way to be right and good, or clone theory of manifestation. Sugmad is infinitely creative and acts as such with torrents of love and manifestation. To be as Sugmad, soul is challenged to reach and stretch into the different frequencies to know more about Sugmad's and souls' abilities to learn and utilize Universal Soul Movement. In some places the "veils between the worlds" are thinner, allowing for easier Universal Soul Movement, and conversely, in some quadrants of creation, life has become too dense and painful. Many souls have failed to realize that much of the density of their perceptions is of their own making. One of the greatest gifts of Sugmad to Its creation is the infusion of Light and Sound in all arenas, all souls, throughout all time and space and far beyond any of these. To aspire to increased awareness and utilization of this is to move beyond mere appearances and limitations to come into one's own Godhood within the grand body of Sugmad.

## Why the development of all intelligent life is directly affected by the "facsimile alignment" of each spiritual body

Facsimile alignment is a direct response to thoughts, beliefs, social conventions, religious teachings, and other such things that are not the truth of the Living Spirit, but are lesser or dead energies. Change the shape of a thought, emotion, or other physical manifestation, and that thing looks different, like a flat piece of paper rolled or folded in many different ways. Through Universal Soul Movement, soul can move anywhere in space and time and be guided to what he or she wishes and needs to learn. Research libraries exist and are opened to the pure of heart with important tasks to do. Life in various stages and various historical figures can be intimately experienced due to the underlying interconnectivity of Spirit and all souls. Hence, souls can move past conventional facsimile alignments to learn from another without the barrier of the mind and emotions or across the barriers of each soul's experiences. That is why it has been crucial for various saviors and savants to teach using images to create a facsimile alignment that can be followed after they are no longer physically available so souls can carry on their work and continue to grow. The use of imagination as a creative frequency emanating from Sugmad to manifest life is the same in the soul body of all life forms, although it is used uniquely by each soul. Intelligent life can easily use this faculty for the good of all. For example, we can see all around us how souls use facsimiles for their own selfish, destructive ends. Some will see perfection as an army marching perfectly in tune and alignment with one another. Yet when souls in some societies eliminate their focus on their problems, everyone is uplifted and the trajectory of souls' awareness exponentially expands. When souls focus on the love in their hearts for Sugmad, instead of thoughts of what they have experienced or need to do in the future, everything changes and souls shift into a higher plane of awareness. Anything less brings a vicious cycle and a large measure of imbalance. Any imbalance brings pain. The moment people stop learning truths from their experiences they start dying. Hence, the development of all intelligent life is directly affected by the "facsimile alignment" of their spiritual bodies.

## Why there is so much focus and attention on the "Revelations" section of the Christian Bible

First of all, there is a lot of money and power to be gained for those who direct others to do so. Secondly, focus and attention on the "Revelations" section of the Christian Bible in recent years has been due to the hopelessness humankind faces when their vision is clouded by tangible reality; they think physical reality is evil or wrong and the Lord of the Lower Worlds is a menace. Fear of annihilation when indulging in profane action and hope of final redemption by an all powerful God appeals to the mind, but also blocks untrained minds that desire to fulfill the promises of being able to enter the New Jerusalem, which dwells in God's heart. Revelations presents a preview or culmination of covenants made and broken, collectively and individually. It is the climax of Biblical prophesies, a lens given to John the Apostle two thousand years ago through which to make sense of promises that were to come. He said it would come soon, but it has been 2000 years - hardly soon to those who await Christ's return by descending on clouds heralded by angels. Concrete thinking Christians have been waiting a very long time for these eminent promises to be fulfilled. Unfortunately, when revelations from the prophets of old are taken literally, distortion clouds the vision of possibility and true meaning of the revelation. Revelations was a code presented to John in a dream, a message to seal the faith and fate of worshippers of the Christ. Remember that much is lost in the translation of Inner experiences to words; the degradation accelerates in the many subsequent translations leading to modern languages of cultures foreign to John and his times. This is a double-edged sword. Fear and hope are actions one must take. Neither is as positive as needed to gain entry and stability into the New Jerusalem, or Sugmad's Inner Worlds. To gain entry, one must rid oneself of all dross connected to fear, anger and attachment to material reality, and replace those thoughts with movements of love. This, of course, is contrary to the fear evoked in Revelations. Soul alone may enter the heart of Sugmad, as is alluded to in Revelations. What needs to be slain is not the physical body, but all thoughts that are not of love but full of Sugmad's grace. Each soul that lives in and channels the heart of Sugmad's love is worthy to open the seals of the scrolls of wisdom in freedom and sail the Inner cosmic seas for eternity, without the outer plagues and trauma earned by souls who reject the Living Love of Sugmad that pours forth for all to drink at all times.

## Why John the Apostle wrote his message of Revelation in a code known by those teachers of the Light and Sound

John the Apostle wrote his message of Revelation to comfort Christians who suffered for their faith in a code known only by teachers of the Light and Sound. He used the most vivid earthly language and symbols he could imagine to evoke images of great impact to impart certain truths beyond the reach of normal language and thinking to strike a chord within the souls not reachable by the mind. How else could he transmit the most extraordinary events that will follow when souls accept or reject the glory of Sugmad? Teachers of the Light and Sound know from personal experience, rather than from logic or deduction, that which is being transmitted by word through this colorful text. Does a beast with ten horns and seven heads mean a literal physical creature or an omniscient menace most fearsome for its power? Forbidden secrets lay imbedded within this secret code known only to those trained and able to reach deep into the Inner Worlds, to be revealed by observing the Our Father's ways, including the Law of Silence. This strategy was not lost on the ruling power of the day; it created confusion and a mystical threatening aura around him, which ensured John's longevity in a time when the life of Christians perched precariously before the vicious opposition who wished to kill any spark awakened in the souls of men by the Christ, for their own security of earthly treasure and power. As such men sought to understand and take advantage of the time when his predictions would manifest they preserved John's right to walk the Earth so they might gain his knowledge. To those who seek material gain, fear is a powerful motivator.

## How the role and secrecy of both Mother Mary's and Mary Magdalene's burial places and bodies play into these changes of world consciousness

The bodies of Christ and true saints, such as Mother Mary and Mary Magdalene, contain certain frequencies and energies that stay within the cellular structure even after the soul has departed. When these great beings walked the Earth with their highly evolved souls inside, the pure energies they channeled changed the very DNA of their physical cells, so that the highest God Power could reside within them and not destroy the cellular structure and make the mind go mad, as it would in beings of lesser training and abilities. Whether this is true is a matter of debate by the mind but truth on certain higher levels we will not disclose here. For those who wish to know the truth of this, ask the Living Sehaji Master or other ascended masters. They must show you; no living being of lesser stature would be able to impart truth beyond the wisdom contained. Certain secret societies have been obsessive over their possession because they wished to ascertain secrets the living beings held when they walked the Earth. This path has been entrenched throughout the history of the last two thousand years. The energies that pass through physical structures at the moment of their creation and thereafter will continue to live within the cellular structure of the physical shell, even in inanimate objects. As artists, musicians, poets and dancers come to know, perceptive lovers of their work will absorb the energies they felt as they created their work, even centuries later. The signature of the structure is set; hence those who are not aware that they can get it directly from Sugmad seek it from others, even the dead relics they leave behind. This is the reason the burial places of Jesus of Nazareth, his mother and wife need to be protected, so that their remains can rest in peace and not be disturbed by those who wish to rob them of their dignity and life energy.

## Why "Armageddon" is a change in world consciousness and not to be construed as the end of the world

Armageddon is the annihilation of thought processes and systems that have too long held souls of the Earth in bondage to the ideas and power of a few for their personal pleasure and gain. When enough people have taken their spiritual maturity seriously, they will begin to awaken to the richness and vastness of the worlds within their hearts, to their connection to life predicated on their own actions and surrender to Sugmad, to their lessons that need to be caught, learned, and integrated, and to the plethora of masters who await their earnest attention. Then we will see a substantial change in world consciousness. Such an event would seem catastrophic to fear mongers and status quo keepers. Revelations called for the end of the world to be coming soon, but as we can see two thousand years later, this has not been physically the case. Great change has already happened in the interior worlds of countless individuals, whose silence about the direct connection eludes the detection of the profane.

## The deeper significance of the numbers "666"

Three sets of six awaken soul's consciousness and break up deep seated patterns of facsimile alignments that have hardened into dead ideas and systems that govern the minds of the inhabitants of the planet. When purposefully placed within the body consciousness, three equilateral angles and sides of each triangle of the six points seen at once in the star tetrahedron awakens the Third Eye gateway and all chakras to energy flows into and out of the physical body, as the Gates of Heaven. Knowledge and use of this gives individuals such freedom, and the freedom souls gain is very threatening to the conventional mind and the priest craft who have subjugated the sacred works of the prophets and Christ for their personal gain.

## How the scientific works of Rife and Tesla ventured into new frontiers only known by other life forms

The brilliant scientific works of Royal Raymond Rife and Nikola Tesla far surpassed the understanding and accomplishments of other scientists of their times, and stretched the awareness and vision of the men and women of their generation and generations to come. They worked hard to discover and live the dreams of other sentient life forms that came before them, and created dreams for those who came after, and are yet to come. Both men paid a high price for their pioneering works of genius. To more advanced life forms, humanity was not ready for their scientific works because of the petty jealousies and greed of the scientific and business establishments. A solid moral foundation needs to be laid for great inventions, because ordinary men tend to follow in the footsteps of others, rather than pave their own trail. Today, the world has had many scientific successes, but gross failures in leadership are guiding the lemmings of the world over the cliff of self-annihilation. It is time to change the path that humanity is following or risk catastrophic wars that will leave the Earth reeling, even worse than the Dark Ages of centuries ago.

World-renowned Serbian-American inventor, physicist, mechanical and electrical engineer Tesla made abundant revolutionary contributions to the field of electricity and magnetism in the late 19th to early 20th century. Tesla's patents and theoretical work shaped a foundation for modern alternating current (AC) electric power systems, including the AC motor. He conceived the induction motor and began developing various devices that used rotating magnetic fields, for which he received patents in 1888 (the year Rife was born). An eccentric genteel genius, Tesla contributed much to the fields of robotics, ballistics, computer science, nuclear physics, and theoretical physics. He worked hard for, was betrayed by, and then rivaled Thomas Edison. Tesla earned his first million by age 40, but inept at finances, he gave away almost all his royalties on future innovations and ripped up a contract with Westinghouse that would have made him the world's first billionaire. Tesla died in poverty at age 86. Although the Nobel Prize in Physics in 1909 was awarded to contested rival Marconi for the radio, the U.S. Supreme Court upheld Tesla's patent after his death in 1943, recognizing him as the inventor of radio. His genius came with a heavy weight that would have crushed other men.

By 1920, Rife had built Planet Earth's first virus microscope, and by 1933, he had constructed the remarkably complex Universal Microscope, with nearly 6,000 dissimilar parts, capable of magnifying objects

60,000 times their size. He became the first human to actually see a live virus. Rife cured many people of cancer safely, without radiation or drugs, by identifying individual spectroscopic signatures of invisible microbes and rotating quartz prisms to focus light of a single wavelength upon his targeted microorganisms, due to their unique signature frequency. It is now an established fact that atoms form molecules when held together with covalent energy bonds that emit and absorb their own specific electromagnetic frequency; hence, each molecule oscillates at its own distinct frequency. No two species of molecule exhibit identical electromagnetic oscillations or energetic signatures. Resonance amplifies light in a similar way, much like ocean waves intensify one another when they merge. Rife's genius caused panic in the hearts of moneymakers in the pharmaceutical and medical communities, which led to his and other supporter's untimely deaths as well as the premature deaths of countless millions to follow, who had to rely solely upon dangerous treatments that brought power to providers instead of healing to the sick. Humanity has been given several cures for cancer, but chooses instead to keep the money generating wheels turning to benefit the few. Rife's work shows the wise that raising consciousness and energetic frequencies will keep the body cancer free and healthy, unless it is their karmic retribution that must be paid or lessons learned for the good of the sick person and attending souls. Routes to health abound in this world filled with dangers for those who have the ears to hear, eyes to see, and hearts to comprehend and open to the Greatest Healer of All.

## Why natural catastrophes are a part of this Earth's planetary contract toward a progressive change in climatic conditions and plate shifts of landmasses

The Earth is dynamic, and ever has been since it was born, in order to birth into its sphere life forms moving in progressive changes in consciousness. An inert or dead planet would only be able to house souls who could not progress in consciousness. Therefore, natural catastrophes are part of this Earth's planetary contract toward a progressive change, which manifests in climatic conditions and plate shifts of landmasses. The consciousness of humans and the consciousness of the planet are inextricably linked; one greatly affects the other. Sickness in societal attitudes brings sickness onto the Earth and its "lower" life forms. The consciousness of the inhabitants of Earth has accelerated, in some ways forward and some ways retrogressively. Without change, growth would cease and all organisms upon the planet would die. Growth equals life. No change equals death. In its quest to survive physically, the human consciousness seeks the security and comfort of non-change. Since there is no life without change and the human consciousness resists change, the natural order brings about forced change manifested in natural catastrophes, which catapult the individual and collective consciousnesses into new arteries of action, which course stronger through the trajectory of spiritual growth mandated by Sugmad for soul's return to Its heart and protection. Since humans cherish comfort and disregard the negative ramifications of their greedy use of natural resources and disregard the natural equilibrium on the Earth as well as in governments, societies, and homes, they in essence say to Sugmad that they need interventions of great magnitude to gain their attention to return their focus to intentional action in right directions, that of energetic growth toward wholeness and equilibrium. It is not only the physical disregard of harmony and equity that are causing climatic conditions and landmass plates to shift; the phenomenon extends into all the Inner Worlds as well. Modern day inhabitants of Earth are generally lazy or hyperactive in greed, emotional immaturity, attachment, lust, taking advantage of one another, and mental disharmony. This sick collective consciousness disturbs the Earth and will destroy it if not mended. Catastrophic shifts will awaken many souls to their true purpose, as they are forced to their knees to surrender and return to natural humility, then rise to their feet to help their brothers and sisters.

## What individual God seekers can do to prepare themselves for the ongoing and upcoming world changes

The quietude or noise of the outside of your life right now reflects you - your Inner peace or turmoil. Notice in this and other moments throughout your day what happens all around you and your response to it. Life mirrors you as much as you mirror life; it is a constant dance and interplay of energy and consciousness or unconsciousness. Give the love to others that Sugmad pours into you; mirror the face of the Divine in the quietude of your heart and mind, without words. Learn to live in a constant state of love, give up complaining, and observe the Law of Silence about your hardships and Inner lessons. Walk through the valley of life with your loved ones and neighbors, with spiritual armor on - impenetrable invisible shields that allow the tremendous love and energy of Sugmad to flow into and through you, but do not allow the unsavory darkness of others to invade you. Yes, there is more than one shield. Upliftment in consciousness now builds a solid base for your future and for those around you, much more than money in the bank or under the mattress, extra food and blankets in the cellar, or other preparations for catastrophe. Changes will not come as you imagine. Your consciousness is the only asset you own. You must stay ever open and vigilant to Sugmad's whispers and messages, not those of your ego or mind, and act on your highest Inner guidance immediately without question.

Contemplate now: Ask Sugmad for help and imagine His refined energy, Light and Sound, love, guidance, and protection flowing into your heart in great and balanced measure. Put in place a permanent Sugmad shield around you. Let only Sugmad's energy permeate the Inner altar of your beingness. Take up the sword of Sugmad, the energy needed to proceed each day without getting drained, and the face of love to have and know the serenity you deserve, the acceptance of reality without resistance, the courage and awareness it takes to change what you can, and the freedom and the wisdom to know what you need to do next. Live in present time. You may want to remember, contemplate, and repeat the simple yet powerful prayer of Alcoholics Anonymous, the Serenity Prayer: "God, grant me the serenity to accept the things I cannot change, the courage to change the things I can, and the wisdom to know the difference."

## A spiritual mantra that will develop personal insights into the God seeker's immediate surroundings and environment

As I told a young lady this morning: Let your crown, mind, and throat open only to the Light and Sound and movement of the Holy Spirit as it moves you. Let no words of ego or power cross your loving lips. Let the day dawn over you and wash you in color splendid and never let a storm linger long enough to soak you to the bone again. Come out of the rain into the dawn at any time throughout the day, for it is ever radiant in God. Find it and go there. Live there for as long as you can and return as frequently as you wish. Stay present. Focus and live in the now. You may ask, "Show me thy ways, Lord," and sing the mantra: **"SING ME VA HAIL YA."**

Remember always - the heart is mightier than the sword.

♥ ♥ ♥

# Chapter Seven

## The Power of Silence

♥ ♥ ♥

*Silence is not a void, as the mind may conjure, but a reservoir full of energy and potency, waiting to be mined by adventurous souls.*

♥ ♥ ♥

## Why teachers of the Light and Sound speak and write about the power of silence

Everything in all the worlds is comprised of energy. No matter exists in the higher worlds and little exists in the physical world. Energy reigns and control of energy is everything. Control is what all humans seek without knowing the proper manner to do so. One of the main things many citizens of the modern, commercialized or "developed" cultures of Earth dread most is silence. Silence equals power and the control of energy, but the process of containment can initially be most uncomfortable. Citizens of the modern cultures on Earth crave comfort the most, hence they miss gaining true power due to avoidance of discomfort. Silence and stillness pervade the Inner Worlds. Silence is not a void, as the mind may conjure, but a reservoir full of energy and potency, waiting to be mined by adventurous souls. Conversely, the ego mind of man loves to be acknowledged, perceived as great, loved, revered, and heralded from the highest rooftops and powerful media airwaves for its accomplishments, its awareness, its power, and its might. The ego mind of modern man loathes and fears being silent. One of the great paradoxes of the worlds of duality is that power can often be found in the most unlikely places. Those places seem to have nothing - no money, no weapons, just secrets. Nothing begets everything. In silence dwells calm, soothing peace, comfort and rest; from rest springs action; from silence springs great creativity and the Breath of God. Silence holds unfathomable power in its bosom, waiting for the patient lover to gently unfold its treasure.

## The secret of the Law of Silence

Learn to cultivate silence. Practice for extended periods of each day by sitting in silence. Be aware only of the present moment and the quest you wish to explore. All answers lie in silence's shadowy depths, which await each adventurer's arrival and exploration. Your Inner chambers within hold total silence; they are filled with all the directions to any situations from which you seek relief. This treasure house within you is the birthplace of manifestation. All energy, all life forms, all conception and gestation happen in the unformed silent recesses of the interior worlds each person holds inside. Humans come to Earth to play out the lines of energy and force that they as soul have been traveling prior to birth, and to manifest their mission and dreams. Somehow, many people become turned around in their use of silence and noise: they fear silence and talk about anything and nothing just to fill the uncomfortable silences, complaining endlessly about problems, which only serves to exacerbate their tribulations and suffering. Learn to love the silence within, as do the spiritual masters. The furnace for creation of all the worlds lies in silence to fuel living creatures born into the Physical Plane and to destroy dross. Learn to wield silence for your advantage. Spiritual masters have learned through much trial and error to exercise this most powerful Law of Silence, to use it for maximum advantage in manifesting the Best-Laid Plans of Sugmad. You can learn to use it too, by recognizing its potency and applying it to your daily life. Learn to be devoted to silence, for it contains the Light and Sound of Sugmad, your most potent ally.

## How the effective use of silence can improve the God seeker's overall life

The Spiritual Hierarchy has gathered together for a new cause, working in conjunction with Dan Rin to move souls forward more rapidly to achieve Sugmad's Best-Laid Plans of seeing more souls enter the kingdom of God in this lifetime in full consciousness and help others to do so as well. Energy is energy and cannot be created or destroyed by soul or man, as science has so clearly shown. Everything uses some form of energy. Humans waste much energy on mindless (or mindful) chatter, on rapture of the trivial, for whining and blaming, and on foretelling what has not been. This causes endless mental and emotional spinning, depression, mind racing, anxiety, externalization of problems to avoid taking responsibility, anger, hatred, violence, death, and perpetual suffering. These are the methods of unaware and hurting souls. Knowing that energy pervades all created and uncreated realms helps awakened souls remember the huge storehouses of potential available for their use. This energy and variations of energetic frequencies are available to anyone. Silence contains energy. The more one remains silent, the more energy builds. Soul need only learn to use the methods and tools of the spiritual realms to manifest energetic frequencies into the mental, emotional, and physical realms. Instead of getting caught in a negative swirling vortex of power created by fear or blaming self or others, stop the cycle and do something different. Learn to transform your swirling internal emotional energies into power generated to accomplish tasks that will move you in the direction you do wish to go. Energy is energy. It is neutral. You can use it for Universal Soul Movement, for exploration of answers, for acquisition of knowledge, awareness, internal experience, and for the accomplishment of tasks that fulfill life missions, contracts, dreams and goals. Stop draining and wasting energy. Instead, learn to transform energy available to you, within you, to your advantage.

## How the proper use of silence incorporates the highest aspect of love for others

Love is the basis of energy pouring forth from God at all times. It pervades the Spiritual Current of Light and Sound that floods all creation. Since silence contains powerful energies with love as its basis, Souls can focus on love and their own heart centers to open the gateways within. To engage in, find comfort in, and survive in the powerful God energies discussed herein, soul must channel all energetic frequencies through the heart of his or her physical shell, letting all that is not love dissipate in the tremendous shower pouring forth. All energies circulate in waves and cycles. What goes forth returns to its sender. What goes around comes around. Loving others is vital to the maintenance of the higher energetic flows so as not to hurt any souls in the path of the energy flow. When awakened souls work to discipline their methods, viewpoints, movements and experiments, they will quickly learn that love is the easiest, sweetest, and most enjoyable path. Love all without judgment, for judgment puts unnecessary and harmful conditions on love, instead of letting it be the cleanser and healer it already is. Let love pour through your heart, purify your heart, and gently rain nourishment on the dry and thirsty souls who crave it. Keep all this in silence to retain your potency, your balance, and to avoid fear and rejection.

## How silence can be used for our "Inner communications" with other souls

The human mind connects soul to memories, emotions, and the physical vehicle that allows it to operate on the Earth. However, the mind of modern man seems to firmly believe in outer manifestations more than Inner realities and truths. Since each person is connected to Spirit and God through the heart, but has a unique history of experiences and genetic material through which to filter these, silence is often the best way to avoid direct confrontation, arguments, rejection, and suffering. The key to remember is that the mind is revered and relied on by most, but the mind is only a tool, not the source of wisdom, love, and truth. Instead of outer talking, which engages the mind and too often shuts out soul and truth, try the art of Inner talking from the silence within, from your heart to theirs, bypassing the mind and its censors and limitations altogether. The Spiritual Hierarchy wants to do the best it can to bring forth the higher truths, love and energy to you to be used to move all of creation into realms of love, stability, happiness, awareness, growth, and more. Only through keeping much of what we know in the realms of silence to avoid debate and debasing of potency can we communicate truths far beyond the mind's ability to grasp and use. The spiritual conveyors in Sugmad's hierarchy speak with you all the time using the silent airwaves, but you rarely tune in to receive their communications. Now you are being told to tune into radio GOD by allowing the energy of God to flow unimpeded through your receptive heart, into your body and life and out again through your transformer heart into the hearts of others. You can extend the range and transmission of higher messages by Inner talking to those you love in your family, workplace, and community. You are wasting time by not doing this every moment of the day.

## How silence opens the heart for the God seeker to speak with the various spiritual masters and archangelic hierarchies

Fear closes the heart; love opens it. Silence opens the Gates of Heaven to allow the flow of spiritual energies into the Loving Heart for the God seeker to speak with any of the various spiritual masters and archangelic hierarchies who have made new agreements to allow access to them directly. The physical universe is fully mature now, but lagging behind in its spiritual cohesiveness and awareness of its duties to return the cycle of energies for highest good, due to squandering its energies, power, and love for personal gain through non-observance of the Law of Silence. Science shows it is harder to get something to flow into a vacuum than into a container with something already inside. Spirit flows more readily into a transparent, selfless, silent heart that contains its potent spiritual current already, than one devoid of that current.

## Why the ancient Greek philosopher and mathematician Pythagoras requested silence of his students during the hour of 9 o'clock

Pythagoras requested silence of his students during the hour of nine at both morning and evening for many reasons. First, he understood the importance of the Law of Silence and the discipline it takes to learn to handle the powerful energy flows that come from silence. The incredible strength needed by soul and the outer bodies to handle the power of Spirit as It comes rushing through bodies unprepared for Its magnitude would weaken, unbalance, and damage an unprepared vehicle, and could even kill a person, if the spiritual current were to pour forth too raw and undiluted. Two hours per day in regular and steady measure, meter, and rhythm provided time and focus to prepare. Secondly, Pythagoras understood, explored and mastered the rhythms and harmonies of numbers in correlation to musical notes. Each of these two hour blocks of time per day shaped a sacred space within his community for holding, exploring, breathing, singing mantras, and other innovative Inner pursuits before and after additional periods of outer active creative expression. These hours of rest, rejuvenation, and retaining huge spectra of intensive vibration and awareness of powerful energies would feel to his students like a dam ready to burst after restraining a reservoir exceeding its capacity. In learning to keep silent, students learned to tap into the greatest reservoir of all, far beyond the capacity of the mind to analyze, criticize, and explain. Thirdly, holding the number 9 within the Third Eye is a powerful mantra which sets up a powerful vibration that reverberates throughout the entire spiritual-mind-body system in both the individual and collective souls who practice techniques together. Into such a matrix, the Inner Master would pour forth lessons and exercises for students to explore their individual and collective Inner Worlds. From years of practice, students built a storehouse of awareness and creativity that propelled the renaissance of Pythagoras' day within their walls and teachings.

## The secret behind the relationship of nine and the use of silence

Again, there are many secrets that build the universes and numerical systems. The number three (3) conveys the primary relationship of the great inflows of energy and power from the unified God Worlds into the lower worlds and into the Physical Plane. It represents the splitting of the one into positive or active, negative or receptive, and neutral or non-power, the sustaining power of the Holy Spirit. The number 9 sets up a rhythm of 3 within 3. Only within the holding of energies can a powerhouse be contained and used to fuel action. A drop of water holds little energy; an ocean holds tremendous amounts of ecosystems, potency, and power. Only in silence can the glory of God begin to be realized, explored and known. In the exploration and utilization of this vast storehouse of Spirit, the mind and heart of humankind can be opened to purge the past of stored, twisted and hurtful engrams. Then, freed of restraints, these clear vehicles can be propelled into action to move forth the dreams of all of the beings who inhabit the Inner and Outer Worlds to achieve Best-Laid Plans.

## Why so many teachers of the Light and Sound have been concerned about their students breaking this valuable Law of Silence

Pythagoras was concerned because he wanted his students to continue with their creative explorations and expanding abilities, which would have dissipated should they have ceased their exercises in silence. He knew that soul learns best through its own experience, rather than by being spoon fed continually, even from the Living Master. Balance between the Inner and Outer Worlds is required for the process of unfoldment to continue and grow. Pythagoras and other teachers of the Light and Sound know that talking spends, dissipates, and wastes energy that must be focused and sharpened in order to be productive. In addition, the petty minds and egos of people lacking in these disciplines and awareness stand by ever present, jealous of, and ready to destroy what they cannot have, due to the negative polarization of their nature and position, whether they are aware of these tendencies or not. Much is revealed in silence that cannot be explained or revealed to the common mind, and such knowledge and wisdom would upset the uneducated mind and social conventions that are not prepared to understand and utilize the revelations and practices contained therein. As the forces of creation, destruction, and non-power make up the stream of Spirit ushering forth from the God Worlds continuously, secrets that need time and space to incubate and grow would be too easily destroyed by those eager to seize power for themselves in a seemingly quick and easy way. The consciousness of soul drives the actions of its lower bodies. Many people in their various developmental stages have been unaware of the gross or subtle forces within their consciousness that are triggered and released through any number of actions and reactions within their own selves and in response to the words and actions of others. Only in silence can the tender shoots of growth be guarded against the potential onslaught of the storm awakened in a weakened soul who has not mastered what another soul is beginning. Each soul must guard its growing awareness and share only some of what it learns with its teachers. Share nothing with those who do not understand or care of that which you speak. Most gifts of consciousness must be held in total silence to garner and use their potency. Each soul is unique and gifted with a unique mission, sensory apparatus, and historical influence; you must guard your gifts and save them for service to the Great God who gave you life.

## How theology and metaphysics are similar to mathematics in thought-structure

Theology, metaphysics, and mathematics are based on certain principles, arrangements, and organizational structures that issue forth from the Mental Plane. There are constraints and rhythms to each as they define their unique arenas of being. Each is comprised of creation, sustenance, and diminution or elimination principles with cadence, tension, and battles fought within. Compare this to the spiritual realities of Sugmad beyond the Great Divide where only unity and oneness reign, where no opposition or destruction exists because all is unified, harmoniously balanced, and inseparable. One cannot think about the God Worlds to experience them. This is why they are rarely addressed in any discipline, as opposed to the way one can think about, analyze, and compare principles set forth in theology, metaphysics, and mathematics, which invite argumentation and division.

## Why silence is the most efficient means of spiritual and conventional communication

The mind complicates things, as it interprets, analyzes, and categorizes. It changes what it perceives according to the consciousness of the soul who uses the mind and mental structures it prefers. Add to the mind an ego structure, which combines the mental, causal and emotional bodies, and the result is a mixture generally too aberrated and one-sided to perceive pure truth, especially if the communicated verbal or written truth is counter to the desires of any of these bodies. Any attempt of these aberrated bodies to communicate brings a twisting of truth to suit the desires and needs for those bodies to feel good about who they are, what they choose to do, and to merely survive. Soul is accustomed to silence, but the mind is not, especially in modern technologically advanced cultures where its citizens are not used to the natural cycles and ups and downs of life. In order for the pure truth of a message to be conveyed, it is best for soul in its purity to do the conveying. Soul is the divine spark of God within people, the part of man that simply *knows*. When a soul sends messages through the medium of silence, through Spirit as the communicator, other souls will pick up the messages; they will bypass their minds and transmit directly soul-to-soul and heart-to-heart. This method of communication is quick, efficient, and great training for all souls involved.

## How the ways and means of silence can be interpreted through the use of hands, eyes and physical demeanor

Words can convey only a small spectrum of truth, since words must go through the mind and the filter of the ego. For many people, words contain little in the way of truth.

Watch instead for the body language of others as they speak and proceed through their day. Tension conveys a conflict; fidgeting and twitching convey nervousness and anxiety. These signals indicate the transmission of something very difficult to reveal, and contain lies and denial. The shaking of the head “No” when the words say “Yes” reveals much of the ambiguity or falsehood of what is being communicated. Each person has developed a set of motions and habits unique to that person, so I cannot give you too many details. If you watch others carefully, after declaring yourself to be a vehicle of God’s love without judgment, and maintain clarity of mind to understand this process, you will begin to denote discrepancies in words and physical demeanor. Observe all body and facial muscles and make note of what you see without judgment, but with simple curiosity; you will begin to learn a new language being spoken. Does the speaker smirk or look smug? Do his or her eyes look veiled or are they darting? Refine your powers of observation for a month or two and much will be revealed. Pay attention to your own body and face when you talk. If you find you are also tense or fidgety, ascertain where the discrepancy lies within your heart. Does your heart align with your mind and body? If not, notice, contemplate and vow only to speak when truth may be revealed. As stated earlier, many truths must be held in silence to maintain purity and potency. Stop wasting this precious energy within you just to feel more comfortable. Part of your spiritual training is to discern truth more minutely and to contain the energies being poured from the higher realms into your lower bodies. This training is vital and will take you to heights unachieved before.

## How silence insures a higher facility of the transfer of knowledge into the mental body

Due to the contingencies of free will, each person is charged with making his or her own decisions and interpretations. The ego, mind, and internal censor easily interfere with free will when inundated with societal mandates and obligations to uphold a certain image. Using communication through the Inner channels in silence conveys pure soul-to-soul and heart-to-heart transmissions with all aspects of the message intact. Many features of any communication that might be conveyed verbally or in written form that must transfer through the mind will be lost if left to the highly creative censor that stands guard over what the mind is charged to handle. This is not so different from the fact that any intermediary medium of transference will distort the purity of an original transmission. For example, when an artist copies an original work of art, some quality is lost with each reproduction, even when done with greatest care. Musicians understand that the full range of sound, especially that part of the spectrum that the ears cannot hear but soul can perceive, is lost in recordings, even with the finest equipment available on Earth today.

When in contemplation, notice as levels or intensities of energy begin to shift inside you. Observe your body's responses. An increase in energy is thought by many to indicate boredom, nervousness, or an inability to sit still and "get it," when in reality, the higher energies from the God Worlds are opening up inside and beginning to pour forth. Instead of getting up, this is precisely the time to remain still and go deeper inside with open receptivity and growing awareness and a resolve to gain and retain what you are receiving. The mind and lower bodies are created as receptacles for this God energy. You can warehouse a tremendous amount of energy without any mental understanding of any of it for use later in measured doses for easier digestion and more comfort.

Learn to discern and differentiate what is merely the discomfort of change from what is truly an alarm of fear. If you declare yourself to be a vehicle for God's love in all sincerity and devote the time it takes to learn of these few truths imparted, you will find your Inner life escalating in awareness and joy. The Inner experiences you seek will come at the pace you allow and the pace the masters help modulate for you, so you will not get out of balance and destroy your life. Do not fear change. Grow into the higher realms with the Inner Master at your side. Great changes will follow, so be prepared if higher consciousness and devotion to the ways of Spirit is truly what you want. Spiritual mastery is available in this lifetime if that is truly your goal and mission in this life.

## A spiritual exercise that will heighten the use of intuition during focused periods of silence

1. As always, declare your intentions to God to be Its vehicle for loving service into all the worlds in which you live and move and have your being.

2. Invite the Inner Master to guide and protect you.

3. In silence for 30-60 minutes, settle into your heart and/or Third Eye, and sing three rounds of "**HU SHHHH ALL ONE SHHH**" three times.

4. Imagine, open to, and feel the higher energies of God coming into you in great and joyful measure. Receive with an open heart and rejoice in the riches of heaven!

5. Tap into this reservoir at any time.

♥ ♥ ♥

# Chapter Eight

## The Nature of Loving Relationships

♥ ♥ ♥

*In all realms of God's grand creation freedom must be given for love to do God's will in God's way, for freedom and love go hand in hand.*

♥ ♥ ♥

## What love is

Love is the essence, the energetic signature, and the creative expression of the Original Divine Principle, which is often called God. Love's energy fuels all the worlds, creates creation, and manifests whatever it beholds. Love is Pure Spirit and Spirit is Pure Love in its greatest attribute. There would be no life in God's worlds without the all encompassing power of love.

## Why love is the essence of this universe's existence

Love is the greatest power in purity and strength, ever giving and never taking. Love cares only for its full expression. Love is creating and sustaining and is never destructive. The universe is creational, intentional, directional, increasing, and in balance, in order for its continual expansion and continued existence. Love is the reason, the season, and the pleasing principle which all life knows, desires, and needs for its survival.

## Why universal love, as a force emanating from Sugmad, is the most important aspect of humanity's creativity

It is vital for humans to remember that the love pouring through their bodies is universal in origin and intention. As stated above, love from Sugmad is never directed at only one or a limited number of destinations. Sugmad's unconditional love is essential to all life, exists within all living beings, as well as rocks, fire, and all inanimate objects. Love flows from its source, which is Sugmad, through all of creation, and is intended for its free expression to rain its sweet waters for all to behold. Universal Love, not personal love, emanates from Sugmad for the creation and nourishment of all, and is the foundational and most important aspect of humanity's creativity. Soul knows this without question. People feel this without argument. When there is an absence of love, all manner of imbalance and degradation begin to grow and fester. In order for souls to heal from the effects of their choices and actions which result in turning away from love, they must return to love. Humans are innately creative, as individual reflections of the Creator. Any creation that is not full of love takes something from all around it. When you feel something missing, something sucking the life out of you, something draining or fear producing, consider the source and how much love comes from within it. Fear is the absence of love. Hell is the complete absence of love. Power without complete and free love for all, with only unidirectional intention, such as favoring one side over another, is imbalanced, not of God, and devoid of love. In order for humanity to return to its original state of creativity and generative activity, people must let go of fear, anger, hate, and any other focus on emotions or actions devoid of love. Each soul must change the vortex and direction of its own heart, and return to the creative outflow of its true heart, which is creativity and love. At this juncture in world history, souls must do this vital work individually and collectively.

## How love relates to free will

As the greatest power, love cares only for its full expression; any truncation of love results in pain. Love, like life, must be free to grow and expand in order to thrive. Love cannot be contained, being the vital essence of Sugmad in its true and full nature. Any restriction or attempt at restriction only serves to limit its expression. Just as any living organism must be free to pursue its innate nature or render its growth distorted, so the Living Spirit of God, which is love, must be given free will and rein to do God's intention and work. Who can tell God how much sun and rain and nutrients a plant needs to survive and thrive? For any soul to limit and restrain another is to begin the death process. Love must be free and souls must give each other the same freedom God gives, in order for the life essence, which is love, to grow and not stagnate and die. Scientists have discovered that some animals will not mate in captivity; even in the animal kingdom, free will is vital to survival. Infants will die without love and without human loving touch. Children and adults become twisted and distorted without enough love, like a plant becomes limp and lifeless without water. In all realms of God's grand creation, freedom must be given for love to do God's will in God's way, for freedom and love go hand in hand.

## How different spiritual hierarchies in the Inner Worlds regulate love universally through all levels of life and consciousness

Many vortices of power exist in all regions of all the worlds and these vortices must be continually created, maintained, and eventually removed. Spiritual hierarchies in the Inner Worlds regulate all manner of spiritual vortices of universally directed unconditional love in order to sustain the growth of creation in inanimate objects, as well as that of animate and sentient beings. Souls, without proper training, can know nothing about this. To not sustain the tremendous energy flows and power of love would cause the destruction of the balance needed to hold all the forces of energy in check and would force existence itself to come to a quick and painful end. It takes much training from the existing hierarchy to the aspiring student to learn the ways and methods of regulating these vortices of power, which is far beyond the ken of this written material. This training happens in the Inner Worlds, but souls in training must practice in the Physical Plane as well, in order to fully master the principles and disciplines involved. Much of the work is done through the Open

Selfless Heart of the student and the Spiritual hierarchy who seek together to fulfill God's Best-Laid Plans in order to reach all life forms on all levels and states of consciousness. Since Sugmad is energetic conscious love, and its essence sustains all life, many souls are needed to do this work. The spiritual hierarchies are in constant need of aspirants to assist in this huge endeavor, especially now that so many souls live upon the Earth and earthly civilization is perched so precariously close to peril.

## How the path of our beliefs directly impacts the love we receive and how we give love to others

The mind is the gateway of soul and Spirit into the worlds of manifestation and into the Physical Plane. Beliefs are engrained thought patterns, sometimes unrecognized by the conscious mind, but nonetheless these beliefs become the captain at the helm if soul is not awakened and in charge. The path of our beliefs directly impacts the amount and frequency of love we receive and how we transform it through our beingness and give it to others. If we believe we are worthy of love, are a vehicle for God's love, and own our mission to be part of a team of souls who channel God's love into the worlds, then it will be so. On the contrary, if we think we are not worthy, if we believe we need to remain angry, depressed, or fearful of something outside or inside ourselves because this is how we have always been, we will not be able to maintain an open flow of love in and out. Our beliefs are like rudders that steer the ship of our dreams. Believe you are a loving soul who surrenders to God's love; be in the vibration of the highest consciousness; energize this part of reality with all your heart; feel the truth of it, and it will manifest! One way or another, we each birth into this world the fruits of our beliefs.

## What love is between man and woman and how this love becomes a manifestation of God's love for all life

Love between man and woman is and was created to be a sacred expression of divine unconditional love between equal souls united in the presence of the larger Creator God. An intimate relationship is often the most passionate and exuberant of any love. Since unconditional love spans all realms and worlds, the energy can be tremendous, but inexperienced and untrained souls may not have the ability to hold these great energies, which leads to distortion of its expression, and too often to betrayal and murder. The sacred bond created, intended, and built into the DNA of the animal kingdom is not just for procreation; it is for the reunion of opposites, for the giving and receiving, for the blending and balancing of energies and consciousness in service to the greater good. When the union of man and woman is consciously devoted to God and in service to each other and the greater whole, then heaven and Earth will move to see that this love is allowed to create and give its gifts to all within its sphere. In this way, the couple's love becomes a manifestation of God's love for all life.

## Why love between man and woman must come from a state of balanced "giving and receiving"

When two souls decide to unite and express their love for one another, it must come from a state of balanced giving and receiving. Love is not about taking or ownership. The union of a man and woman is about the experience of the love of God bringing two polarities together in a loving way. Balance is required in all things in the worlds of manifestation. If balance is not created and maintained, then all things fall apart. This is one of the fixed spiritual laws in this universe. In balance, a sacred and harmonious union of a man and a woman can be sustained for a lifetime and beyond. Unconditional and passionate love between man and woman must come from a state of balanced giving and receiving, in order to maintain a harmonious equilibrium, a centrifugal force field of energy within a self-sustaining vortex of multileveled energy, to keep the fires burning on all levels of their union. Only by the free will and energetic presentation by both partners can this be achieved. Within this state, a gateway into their created vortex is opened for the non-power of God to come rushing in for both man and woman to experience, partake of and rise into ever increasing levels and realms of energy and consciousness. Herein lies the true ecstasy that mystics have long whispered: union with God through the individual and divine union of male and female.

## The question that should be asked at the beginning of a love relationship

Love's success is dependent on receiving what we cannot provide for ourselves in order to achieve new levels of wholeness and joy. If we could provide it, we would not need and desire the other and would soon tire of and stray from that union. Then the union would dissolve. Many make the mistake of giving or taking too much and throwing off the balance in their loving relationships. We must be willing to receive as well as to give, to allow the partner to give of his or her gifts and in so doing, allow for the vortex to be opened and love to multiply. We would prosper if we would only ask in the beginning of love relationships - "What can you provide for me that I do not already have?" If the person is unable to say, then ask God or the Inner Master to show you the answer to this question. If your potential partner has no awareness of their Inner workings and what they have to give to you, then you might consider if this is the best partnership for you. Certainly all people can learn to go deeper into the God realms to retrieve a truer answer; some may have exactly what you are looking for but be unable to articulate in words. Let the heart ask and listen for the true answer from an Inner soul-to-soul connection. Then before making a life commitment, let the person demonstrate in the coming months what he or she truly has to give.

## How technology is robbing our children of their innocence

Technology robs children of their innocence in many overt and covert ways. In primitive societies, children learn from natural cycles of life. They watch adults manifest food from the ground, usable goods from raw materials, and other provisions for basic needs and enjoyment. They listen to stories at mealtime and ceremonial gatherings told by elders who care about maintaining standards for the survival of their community. Children who watch cartoons and other programs on television, and who play video games, become enamored with fast paced, highly stimulating, sexualized, and violent material. If parents and caregivers reinforce the notion, children may come to understand on an intellectual level that such forms of entertainment are not reality, but merely fantasy. However, on a much more influential emotional level, children do not comprehend this difference. They become physically and chemically addicted to excitement and the hormones coursing through their brains and bodies; they develop no realistic grasp of the threat of danger. Repeatedly exposed to unnatural levels of stimulation created by someone else, children lose or never develop their own natural motivation and ability to create, explore their personal and unique Inner Worlds, listen to the still soft voice within, and surrender to a larger world of spiritual mystery. Life for them becomes a quest for external stimulation, instant gratification, entertainment, and sensual fulfillment - the more the better. Since few can creatively compete with highly paid teams of geniuses that thrive on corporate greed, children may unconsciously believe they are not talented, can never compete, and are not good enough. Cartoons, movies, sports, and news programs expose young minds to too much violence, out-of-context sex, and a general lack of compassion. Winning for thrills, conquering, and annihilating become coveted goals and grand prizes. Hypnotized by mass media, children learn to get one over on the next guy, to win at the expense of all else, to conform to a projected image, to consume, to manipulate, or retreat into their own shells. Through technology, children are given an acceptable way to avoid contact with others, further denying needed interactions that would teach everyone involved how to handle their emotions and energy, refine their communication skills, and generally manage their energy. In the confines of their own little high-tech worlds, safely buffeted from bothering mom and dad, children are now being seen and told they are good and well behaved for appearing docile and compliant. Meanwhile, their social and coping skills are being diminished.

This loss of innocence, imagination, and skill leads to a fragmentary understanding of love between man and woman. Since people are attracted to others of parallel consciousness and frequency, high-tech children are drawn to similar fragmented beings that have never developed an understanding of who they are. Two half beings do not unite to make a whole being. They just know they need something they do not have and want to get it by any shortcut method at their disposal. Their "love" is in reality only an addiction, a need for gratification from an external source. Without self-awareness, discipline, and skills, a man and woman will not be able to live harmoniously together in their full aliveness. Witness how so many couples begin with romance and passionate love, similar to an enjoyable movie, but after a few months, end up taking so much from the other or taking their partner for granted. They are not acting out of love anymore, but out of personal egotistic gratification. Love gives. Taking sucks the vitality out of a relationship. Unconditional love must be the foundation and the building blocks of daily living within any relationship or it will disintegrate.

## How a parent, friend or lover can give of themselves to others to compensate for the love they have not yet received

Everyone needs love. No matter what our role in life, we can nourish others by the simple act of giving love from the heart, without expectations, without strings attached, but just pure love. Like a flower withering in a drought, a person who has not known enough love will feel energized from simple acts of blessing such as a kind word, a smile, or a sincere friendly touch or hug. No matter what a person has suffered, love will open the heart. You may not be able to see it, but trust this and you will feel the effects all around. Simple acts of compassion and caring, kindness and joy, harmony and acceptance will compensate for many slights and traumas known and unknown. Love heals and can be very simply given.

## How premature sex in the development of a loving relationship clouds the perception of compatibility

When searching for a mate, much clarity needs to be maintained over a substantial period of time in order for the myriad of factors needed for compatibility to be clearly known. In the development of a loving relationship, premature sex overpowers the physical and emotional senses and sets up a false sense of Inner connection and compatibility. This strong energetic exuberance is too often misinterpreted as the true deep spiritual love each person seeks in a life partner. The intoxicating after effects of sex clouds the perception of even an experienced man or woman. How could one understand areas of compatibility that require subtle observation and maturity when one is inundated with hormones that strive to be repeatedly experienced? Infatuation feels like abiding love to the immature and vulnerable. This is definitely not enough for a loving relationship to survive the tests of daily life. The drive for procreation is so strong a survival mechanism that the proliferation of neurotransmitters and other chemicals produced by sexual contact completely override the heart and mind's ability to discriminate and make mature and wise decisions. Many a couple has rushed prematurely into a sexual relationship and thought this would bring eternal joy, only to awaken a few months later to the reality that this is not so. Too often commitments have been forged which take years and lifetimes to dismantle.

## How the premature spiritual imprint and release of hormones in the sexual intimacy of a loving relationship often leaves its participants prisoners to passion rather than achieving the enjoyment of a stable love relationship

Lust is one of the most intoxicating emotions and experiences; there is no drug more powerful on Earth than the sexual hormones released in loving passionate sexual joining. Premature sex, that is sexual intimacy prior to true confirmation of exactly who the other person is, what that person is truly capable of being and doing, and their intentions with you and in the world, leaves an indelible spiritual imprint and releases an indiscriminate flood of hormones which mimic the ecstasy found in spiritual union. Such sexual intimation of a loving relationship often leaves each participant a prisoner to passion because subsequent pursuit of even more pleasure overrides soul's more refined needs for the enjoyment of the stability of love. The partners become their lower animal natures in the pursuit of more sex rather than more love, which feels the same. Since the initial peak of sexual passion only lasts so long, when it dissipates, the partners may find themselves in bed with strangers with smelly breath and rude habits overlooked in the peak of passion. When the giving of love so coveted and cherished becomes replaced with faultfinding and withdrawal of attention, partners will be left bewildered, wondering what happened to that love they thought they had found at last. In the wake of waking up, partners find themselves reverting to their old habits. Angry people will become angry and blame the other person. Depressed people will depress themselves once more. Insecure partners will wonder what it is about themselves that failed and become more deeply rooted in their neurosis. If the relationship breaks apart and the partners go in search of another lover and repeat the same pattern, the rut previously experienced becomes more deeply entrenched, until a sense of hopelessness overtakes each person or they continue their acting out in more outrageous and hurtful ways. None of these usual responses leads to the stability of love all souls seek.

## A spiritual exercise that will tune the participant to their potential partner's heart and intention

The first part of this exercise is needed to tune a person to their potential partner's heart. The intention is to know and love their own self, to be in tune with their own heart and desires. This should be done first and foremost before attempting this exercise. For some, this first part may involve a retreat from romantic or sexual relationships, for a time, to reorient to their Inner reality, soul awareness, and life contract.

Once this is accomplished to soul's satisfaction, proceed to **tune into the frequency of love in which you wish to live your life:**

1. Ask Sugmad and the Inner Master to attune you to the correct frequencies of love in alignment with your mission in this life. (This contemplation generally lasts a minimum of twenty minutes.)

2. In the silence of your heart ask a potential partner on the Inner planes what their intention is with you and what their heart's true desire is.

3. Get to know the person on the Inner as well as on the Physical Plane.

4. Ask the Inner Master to accompany you repeatedly to the Inner sanctum where the two of you can meet and converse, with and without words, to ascertain your true vibration and intentions.

5. Ask to be shown clearly and without resistance how to proceed in outward movement toward building or letting go of the relationship.

6. At any time in contemplation or when in the physical presence of the person, you may sing silently "**SAY TU SEE TA SHANTI**" five times. Ask the Oversoul of the person "Are you here to pay a debt, collect a debt, or give and receive mutual love and support for our entire lifetime together?"

7. Keep your heart open to the answer and trust in the wisdom and freedom you will receive.

## A spiritual exercise that will lead you to convey the needs of your heart and emotional expectations

1. After singing **HU** five times, you may say the following or rewrite this in your own words: "Dearest Beloved God, please send a true message of love straight from your heart into mine and into the one I love and wish to know. If this love is best for us on all levels of our beingness, please let us know with clearest certainty. I wish to be happy, to give and receive love in equal measure, and to serve in your Best-Laid Plans, Dearest God."

2. Say and feel this with full passion on all levels of your heart, with emotional expectation and intention and sing: **"OU A SEN TA TU VAIN"** five times and let your heart speak. Your heart will let you know when to open your eyes and give closure to the exercise.

♥ ♥ ♥

# Chapter Nine

## Images in the Mirror

♥ ♥ ♥

*To see yourself as soul is to know and see God's face in yours, hear God's heartbeat in yours, feel God's hand on yours, and to ultimately know God's intention as your own.*

♥ ♥ ♥

## Why the "discovery of self" is so elusive in this world of fleeting appearances

Most people today live their lives in and from their emotional bodies. Trying to live life predominantly from this level of consciousness is akin to a wildly gyrating man stomping out an endless stream of little fires on the ground, burning his worn out feet, but unable to stop in spite of the pain due to his inability to see the futility of his crazy dance. There is another way. Not only does a strongly cultivated hunger for gross stimulation produce lethargy for the fineness of the ethereal, but the "discovery of self" appears to be so elusive in this world of fleeting appearances because people today depend more on outer appearances and confirmations of their beliefs and experiences, due to cultural and karmic influences. They have lost admiration for the wisdom of elders who reminded succeeding generations how to replace the coarse stimulation of emotional and physical realities with the sublime assurance of their true Inner beingness and knowingness by their teaching and examples. As humankind grows in its reliance on technology, it focuses less on its Inner gifts and subsequently loses access to the Inner technologies once developed in revered leaders; now these have become commonly considered ancient, imaginary or non-real art forms. These need to be retained and developed, but have become less accessible as more emphasis is placed on material wealth, entertainment, consumerism, and greed. However, once people delve deeply enough into the material slavery they find has consumed them, they may reach out for help from teachers who are reawakening and able to share what has long been known and taught. The mysteries revealed within these pages are not forgotten unless one chooses to not be aware in this very moment.

## How life changes after God seekers discover their spiritual selfhood and identity as souls

There exists a soothing balm for the blisters of the wild fire dancer. Once a soul discovers his or her true self to be soul and not the mind, emotions, or physical body, the energies of God, Spirit, and the universal Orders come rushing in to celebrate the blessed event. At last, the soul experiences a long sought ecstasy, knowing that the highest vibrations of truth and love come from within and not from anything outside. This discovery awakens frequencies and engrams laying dormant, stimulating every aspect of the person, sometimes so much so that an imbalance can occur, especially if the mind has not been properly trained to understand what is happening. Love pours in so intensely that he or she may seek to do something to dissipate these intense, previously un-encountered energies. Since the mind can be very tricky and unruly without proper training and discipline, he or she may be in jeopardy of committing foolish acts. If the person has been trained under a true spiritual master, the mind will comprehend what the bodies experience once the soul awakens, relaxes, and opens to the higher energies of the Inner God Worlds. Life changes to accommodate the change in consciousness and responds to the new energetic level as long as it is maintained. Life is not necessarily easier for God seekers, as they are continually trained, tested, strengthened, fortified, and trained some more. The God seekers must maintain their balance and focus on compassionate detachment from what they are experiencing. With patience, curiosity and wonder, souls can learn to accommodate the ever-increasing amounts of energies that are now surging through their material bodies. Since like attracts like, souls become like powerful magnets, attracting whatever is held within their consciousness. The soul and mind are now encouraged to continue their purification process by purging the negativity of the past and focusing on the present moment in a deeper fullness. For some, the mysteries of life unfold instantly as their hearts open and their attention shifts to continual wonder, awe, and an ever-flowing feeling of love.

## Why the "discovery of self" is also known as Self-Realization, which is the first stage of heavenly entrance into the Worlds of Beingness and Pure Love

Worlds unlimited exist in God's great creation and plan. Vast are the worlds within worlds created by each soul as he or she moves through the realms of space and time. One must come to know the self as part of the Creator and the creation, as a causeway of the Greater One. Self-Realization is merely the first stage of heavenly entrance on soul's journey into the Worlds of Beingness and Pure Love. To be able to differentiate the true self (called soul) from the clay shell, emotional, causal, and mental bodies as unique and separate yet intimately connected to another is to know that one is far more, can perceive more, and can experience far more than what is seen on the outside of the physical body and known to the collective society that sets a social consciousness. This state of consciousness, known as Self-Realization, is the first stage of true awakening, Inner connection, and freedom, and can therefore be appreciated as the first heavenly entrance into the Worlds of Beingness and Pure Love.

## How the "discovery of self" changes the perceptions that the God seeker emanates and projects to their family and friends

To come to discover what is true and unique about one's self and the creations soul experiences provides growing awareness and compassion for one's self and for others as they struggle with outer appearances or illusions. Once one realizes that soul is the true beingness and is not captive of the worlds in which he or she lives, soul can start to live in the way God intended, as co-creator, as cause and not effect of all outer, coarser circumstances. This changes the way God seekers perceive themselves and the worlds in which they live, which in turn changes the emanation of their frequencies and energy from the centers of their beingness. The "discovery of self" changes how and what soul projects, because soul can now become free of illusion. As the awakened soul breaks free of the constraints and blindness of the social consciousness and his or her own karmic structure, he or she can now choose what to share with his or her family and friends. An awakened soul knows intuitively what is best for all concerned as he or she takes his or her place among other awakened souls and masters to put forward the Best-Laid Plans of God. All lesser concerns drop like dead weights that have outlived their usefulness.

## Why Selfhood is the first reflection of "seeing God's face" in one's self

Selfhood, which is a true and deep knowing that you are eternal soul and a piece of and reflection of God, is truly seeing God's face in your own. God is reflected in every part of His creation, in every soul. God's manifested body projects into all the worlds of Unified Oneness and the lower planes of duality and manifestation. To see yourself as soul is to know and see God's face in yours, hear God's heartbeat in yours, feel God's hand on yours, and to ultimately know God's intention as your own. This is peace and bliss!

## Why self as soul must direct the lower bodies before further movement into the God Worlds is fully established

The God Worlds are precisely balanced in love and wholeness. The entry of any soul must also be balanced in love and intention, with adequate knowledge and expertise in navigating the Inner Worlds and carrying forth soul's and God's aligned missions. When not under the direction of Soul Consciousness, the emotional and mental bodies will find themselves under the influence of the individual's engrams or aberrations gained in sojourns in the lower worlds. The emotional and mental bodies must be trained and learn to follow the direction of soul in order to gain entry into God's finer frequencies, so as to not do harm by upsetting the balance and Best-Laid Plans. Therefore, the higher vibrational planes are carefully guarded and souls are carefully screened prior to being granted entry. Another important reason is that the higher frequencies can greatly upset the lower (mental, causal, emotional and physical) bodies upon soul's return to the lower planes if they are not properly prepared to handle these frequencies. Sugmad wants Its children to see clearly, go with ease and regularity into Its many wondrous worlds, and not hurt themselves or one another. These safeguards are for the good of all living beings.

## How selfhood changes the way we assess and utilize academic and spiritual knowledge in our everyday lives

Once souls are awakened and properly trained to achieve awakened selfhood, they are no longer content to research the interpretations of other souls who have not received that level of training, as one would find in 98% of all physically written materials. At this point, selfhood propels adventurous, eager souls to research for themselves in the Inner Worlds. Happily, libraries, wisdom temples, vortices, and many other places of higher learning flourish on the Inner planes on every level and in every city on each plane. Knowledge and awareness gained in these Inner places is ever kept current and alive, and is ready and waiting for living souls to gain and apply in their own good time. Souls will only be able to access materials and frequencies they can handle and which are assigned to their use. Thus, when souls return with research completed from these Inner adventures, the information gleaned may surprise and even contradict the conventional knowledge of the time and culture in which they dwell. Thus, souls must be awakened and purified to integrate the higher awareness and frequencies within their own context of self and must wisely choose the way such knowledge is utilized, so as not to unbalance or harm themselves or the society in which they live. Many so-called great thinkers such as Nietzsche, Einstein, Da Vinci, and Churchill were actually adept at accessing these Inner realms. Knowledge gained there has propelled great advances in all areas of earthly life.

## Why some philosophers used self-inquiry and rigorous questions to develop selfhood and how this approach leads to the development of one's truth

*Socrates*

Questions open a specific line of inquiry so that detailed knowledge in one direction can be accessed and the flow of Spirit that carries this knowledge can be maintained and developed. Souls need more than general knowledge. In order for an individual to know himself or herself, develop awareness of his or her mission and how to easily and swiftly access what is needed in accordance with the Best-Laid Plans of God, a soul must experiment with and test hypotheses in order to ascertain truth and increase his or her frequency and ability to move forward. Teachers who discourage questions decrease souls' freedom and increase their dependency on another, which is either a sure sign of incongruity and immaturity on the part of the teacher or outright malicious intent to enslave. Questions do form in the mental body, but the proper use of questioning must not be an exercise of the mind. All are encouraged to use the structure and assets of their minds as tools to ascertain truth and refine their progress on their paths. One can never know truth by reliance on the words of others, for this is the way to dependency and slavery. One must develop one's own truth seeking mechanism, test what one experiences, sift through and discard non-truth, and further develop the truth one seeks. I encouraged all my students then and all souls today to finely tune into the divine and relative truths, and to test and retest, if necessary, to thoroughly know and join the souls who inhabit higher realms. The key to questioning is to not get caught up and confined in the realm of the mind, but to stay open as soul in the loving heart and adventurous realms beyond the mind. Finely attuning all receptors on all levels of consciousness will answer any questions the mind can formulate, and help soul to understand the fine complexity and intricate beauty of God and Its creation.

## What the age-old phrase "Know thyself" means

The quest to know thyself is the journey of the ages, for to truly know the true, eternal self is to know a rich and unique aspect of God, who lives in the collectivity of souls and beyond to the unique beingness of God's own nature. Only by determined and pointed adventurous seeking can soul reap the benefit of its numerous experiences, which sharpen perceptions, open and refine the heart consciousness, and allow the fullness of the radiance of God to shine through without imbalance or destruction of Its course and mission. To know thyself is to know the part of God uniquely entrusted to the individual's heart and soul. Without full awareness, only mechanical sludge can come through, which is of little value and delays the Best-Laid Plans of the self and the whole. In addition, to know thyself is the opening to the source of pure joy! Within our hearts lie the gates of heaven.

## A contemplative technique that will give the God seeker a deeper insight into Self-Realization and its importance to spiritual unfoldment

1. Formulate a true and precise question to ask the Inner Master to gain a deeper insight into Self-Realization and its importance to spiritual unfoldment, as the true yearning of your heart and soul.

2. Write the question on the top of the paper, then close your eyes and sing **HU** five times.

3. Sing "**HU LA MAYTA**" three times and **HU** five more times.

4. Then ask your question again, as you envision meeting the Inner Master or your own soul and Oversoul in their radiant bodies.

5. Hold your vision and know this is manifesting as you are creating it within the vision of God that is in you.

6. Focus on your heart center connecting to the heart of God and go deeper into the opening that will follow.

7. If a clear answer does not come, do the exercise daily for seven days, changing and refining the question or techniques as is needed for your true

and unique self. Know that the answers to the question you have asked lie within you.

8. Feel free to refine the question, as you feel nudged to do. Know that as you ask, so you shall receive!

## The intent of this prayer song focuses on the attainment of Self-Realization

1. Sing the **HU** five times and contemplate this prayer, line by line or as a whole.

   ***In stillness****, I know within my heart*
   *That I am needed within* ***God's Will.***
   *Sensing within my most cherished part,*
   *I move in* ***deeper still.***
   *Catching waves of love that are flowing,*
   *Coursing, moving in, around, and through,*
   *My senses reel; I feel it glowing*
   *Frequencies made of* ***HU***
   *For I am soul, and now know this well.*
   ***Being still****, I let go of my past.*
   *I feel such love move within and swell,*
   *As my heart blooms at last.*
   *Trusting my impressions, this is how*
   ***I sing HU*** *and show my place in God.*

2. Conclude the prayer with five more long and loving rounds of **HU**.

♥ ♥ ♥

# *Chapter Ten*

## *Ancient Voices of the Light and Sound*

♥ ♥ ♥

*There is only one path: from dark to light, ignorance to awareness, from reliance on physicality to reliance on the much more dynamic and exhilarating Light and Sound of the Holy Spirit and absorption into God Itself, with subsequent commitment to helping others.*

♥ ♥ ♥

## Why the Light and Sound, in the form of a mystery school now known as The Way of Truth, has migrated from country to country throughout this planet

The Light and Sound is timeless, meaning it is beyond space and time. As souls incarnate in many places, the consciousness needed to bring them forward in their development is offered to many peoples of various countries on Earth, as well as locations elsewhere. Souls must incarnate in many cultures and races in order to experience much variety, learn of different ways of being and situations in order to develop a universal perspective and not get struck in one "right" way of being. The mystery school called The Way of Truth is now moving across the globe as a beacon and wake up call to all souls hungering for the next step in their spiritual journeys. Those souls are ready to do the work Sugmad has planned and needs to be done. No longer are souls called to develop simply for their own self-fulfillment. With increasingly dark forces of hate, greed, rage, and malicious competition careening our planet ever faster toward monetary, military and moral disintegration, many pure bright lights are needed to change the negative vortex of the social consciousness, controlled not by higher principles, but by selfishness and retribution. The bottom line is this: in order to save the Earth as a habitable planet where souls can continue to grow, much movement in consciousness needs to occur now.

## Why there has been so much focus and attention on Africa and its upliftment

Africa has paid long and dearly for its psychic and physical crimes committed many thousands of years ago. Its tremendous vitality and natural resources have been severely exploited by hostile foreign and domestic nations that were wolves masquerading in sheep's clothing. Africa's wealth lies far beyond diamonds and oil. Its true abundance lies in its millions of citizens and their love for family and Earth, survival and community, flexibility and humility. Africa's heart is the wounded heart of our planet, which needs to be healed now. The Way of Truth has come to inspire a loving population to re-achieve its rightful place upon the world stage, with dignity and a new chance.

## Why the ancient masters like Babaji, Abraham, Jesus and Buddha have so much in common regarding their message of love

Love is the core emanation and message of God, taught to all Its children. All spiritual teachers and masters understand this common thread and emphasize love to their pupils in the ways the consciousness of their times can comprehend. The untrained human mind is adept at blocking love and therefore needs a constant reminder to relax and let love in.

## Why every theology and path of life has its own Holy Book and how this affects the consciousness of the group it represents

Each avatar has spoken to the consciousness prevalent among seekers in the forms and languages of their times by using images and stories that were relevant in their day. Unfortunately, not all avatars wrote their messages personally or edited for purity. Their disciples often wrote their teacher's messages and often omitted, did not fully understand, or intentionally twisted the master's words to suit their understanding and aims at social control. The minds of disciples were not as masterful as their teacher's and thus altered the purity of the message given. The mind is like a hungry tiger, powerful enough to accumulate a large stockpile of food, but unable to eat it all, indiscriminate of what is to be eaten or wasted. Love abounds in the many messages of the ancient master teachers, but often gets lost among the pile of extraneous details which once carried the energy and vibration needed to lift souls into the love of which was spoken. Time, cultural change, language translation, and other factors served to distort the intent and focus of the parables delivered, but people hunger for truth and love and will hold onto the words of the avatars they worship and the images and concepts their Holy Books deliver. Slight modifications in words and understated nuances can easily be lost and can change the focus of the meaning in subtle ways that only a highly trained soul would recognize. This is why a living spiritual master is vital to communicate the eternal truths and wisdom of the ages with clarity and purity. Without such clarity, love must be the center and core for the details of the ancient texts to be comprehended in their true perspectives.

## Why the spiritual hierarchies communicate with one another and how they are bonded to each other by the love of the Sugmad

The spiritual hierarchies communicate heart-to-heart and soul-to-soul to further their work and design of Best-Laid Plans. Once soul has achieved mastery in the higher realms, these communications are swifter and purer that those in the physical form. Love and the carrying out of God's plan bonds all to the same goal, as players on a soccer team can be both superstars and teammates. Masters forfeit their egos to serve from their hearts. Once participants learn what is needed and all that can be learned from one path, they are shown or search for another path or teacher to continue into greater awareness, love, and joy. This helps fulfill their life contracts and may even expand those contracts to include goals now achievable. There is only one path: from dark to light, ignorance to awareness, from reliance on physicality to reliance on the much more dynamic and exhilarating Light and Sound of the Holy Spirit and absorption into God Itself, with subsequent commitment to helping others. No enmity exists among spiritual masters, any more than a kindergarten teacher rivals a middle school teacher or a college professor. All true spiritual masters take souls under their guidance for a short time and then send them on their way once they are ready to continue on their journeys.

## Paths of life are not accidental and must fall within the universal plan of Sugmad's contract with existence

There are no accidents among the teachers who walked the Earth and taught the lessons of life to their students. From the very beginning, Sugmad set a plan in place and set the original souls to whom it gave life upon the path of Its preference with full knowledge, awareness, capabilities, and responsibilities to lead others who came behind. All souls must fall within the universal plan of Sugmad's contract with existence, Its own creation. If a teaching is not in alignment with the truth of life, then it will lead the aspirant astray and nothing is more egregious than this. Sugmad has set a plan in place for each soul to have free will and for each soul to experience life in its entirety and learn of many lessons and ways that would help that soul mature into full awareness of himself or herself in all of his or her aspects and abilities. A path invented for self-aggrandizement and personal ambition without full alignment with the eternal truths and contracts laid out by Sugmad would confuse souls and send them on a trajectory far from the design of Best-Laid Plans. One soul can easily be deterred for thousands of lifetimes and start a chain reaction that could deter millions of souls on all levels of beingness. Unfortunately, the contract of free will that souls possess has led many to indulge in greed, vanity, attachment, and personal ambition, and has derailed many an unsuspecting soul. Such misconduct has caused the Earth world to spin out of the positive vortex originally set for it and into a steady decline.

## Why every soul is under the guidance of a spiritual teacher and angelic hierarchy whether they are conscious of it or not

No soul could possibly navigate the rough waters of life without an experienced, loving, and merciful spiritual teacher. Souls have the right, according to their free will, to reject their teacher, to ignore and even vilify the teacher and spiritual hierarchy. Nonetheless, the spiritual hierarchy, like loving parents, stands by watching and waiting patiently for the souls to learn the hard way and return in their own time for help and guidance. Souls are prodigal sons and daughters who, with grace, can learn the tools of the parents to gain their rightful place in the spiritual society.

## Why countries have karmic cycles in the same way individual souls have karmic cycles and how these cycles can result in wars, epidemics and economic depression

Countries, regions, and even planets have karmic cycles in the same way individual souls have karmic cycles. This is little known, but important to understand. All living systems have karmic cycles. Once a trend is set in motion, it takes on a life of its own for a period of time. The more energy initially given and then maintained, the more the cycle will perpetuate. It is much easier to start in a direction and keep going than to change direction once started. Individuals would do well to heed this fundamental law of karma, known also as the Law of Cause and Effect. Once individuals react in a negative way, those reactions cause chain reactions in others who have been affected. If an initial reaction is powerful enough or fed by negative emotional energy, it will continue to grow and fester. Imagine a brotherly squabble that never reaches resolution, but passes down generation to generation, each side polarizing in viewpoint, without the healing balm of reconciliation and love. This illustrates a common igniting spark of war. Once a physical or emotional fire is ignited, fueled, and stoked, it will continue until the fuel is exhausted or a larger force quenches it. These cycles can result in wars, epidemics, and economic depression, as the force of the negative energy moves out into the larger community and continues to fuel animosity in others. Of course, the initial disagreement gets lost as the idea of hatred, injustice, anger, rage, and fear perpetuate and mutate, as is the way of life. Once a fire of great proportion rages on for long enough, the entire system sickens and begins to die, and in doing so poisons other systems created to sustain life. This is how epidemics begin. Not only is the physical world affected, but also all systems on all levels that fuel life manifested on the Physical Plane. Economic depression results from individual and societal depression on all levels, as well. Health cannot come from attention paid strictly to the sickness without the introduction of love and healing energies.

## Why the ancient masters of Earth speak of "space and time" as an illusion and how this perspective affects the human consciousness' sense of reality

The ancient masters of Earth have spoken of "space and time" as an illusion because time and space are merely the effect of an original cause that has become obscured. The cause still exists, but is not acknowledged as the true reality that can be tapped into again and used in a different way with a different force and trajectory. Sometimes it is better to start over than to try to make right a sickened system, akin to the idea: "stop throwing good money after bad." Adding more water to a leaky bucket will not stop the leak but may obscure the problem for a time. Much in life is not seen, but appears to be something other than what it really is. Illusion abounds to the ignorant senses and mind. There is so much more to life and to time and space than meets the eye, the physical measuring devices of science, and the scope of modern philosophical understanding. The common human consciousness perceives reality to be what the senses perceive, or what it is taught or wants to believe, especially if the system has survived the test for long periods of time. The illusion of how things "are" is perpetuated, as commonly understood perspectives are solidified in respected social systems such as academia, science, and "common sense." Some folks now say, "Seeing is believing." Listen to the most brilliant minds of the world argue with passionately opposing views that both appear to make sense when taken as presented without the counterbalancing view. The effect of time is different and unique in each individual's consciousness because their preceptors are fixed to their own vibration and viewpoint. Some say time has flown this year, while others perceive time to be dragging. Does enjoyment make time fly or stand still? What is the effect of pain on your time perception? What happens when you are unconscious versus minutely aware of every moment? Experiment with your own conceptions and perceptions to ascertain the truth of what is given.

## Why happiness is determined by cooperation with and understanding of Divine Will

Humankind's happiness is determined by its cooperation and understanding of Divine Will, because it is God's will for all beings to form alliances, come together and grow in love, change, and increase. Only through cooperation can love really thrive and multiply. Love is God's will and the healing balm that must be core and central for any relationship to be sustained and grow. Only through love, through the union of souls in opposition, can the full range of experience, hardships in life, and the movement away from one's small comfort zone be known, and greater challenges and levels of awareness be faced and mastered. All increases in consciousness are formed by alliances between groups of cells, souls, beings, systems, and communities. It is cooperation that provides the fertile soil for the seeds of new awareness and experience to be nourished and flower.

## The meaning of the concept that "the physical universe is already complete and finished"

All necessary building blocks in the physical universe are already in place from the birth of matter, originating from the so-called "Big Bang." All that is left is rearrangement! Interior and physical universes evolved from the last 15 plus billion years to form many systems, which are ready to be manipulated and enjoyed by souls. Souls, being offspring of the Creator, have an innate ability, the gift of free will, and the mandate to go forth and create. All creations manifest from the inside out. Soul moves through its available universes, stepping through the levels of energetic frequencies and vibrations, from intuitions, to thoughts, through emotional responses, into the physical, moving matter and forming new experiences and creations. It may appear as if new things are being created, but look deeply to see how it is only souls rearranging what is already complete and finished into "new forms." Learning happens and the old appears new when soul moves around and discovers something "new."

## A contemplative exercise with a mantra that heightens insight on areas of life concerns and one's life mission

1. Write your concern or question on the top of a blank page.

2. Ask the Inner Master or God to show you now, or within three days, what is happening in greater depth in some area of your life concerns or life mission.

3. Talk to your mind, as if it were a trusted servant, and send it off in search of the answer. Ask aloud, on paper, and inwardly for help and surrender to what will come.

4. After singing **HU** five times, sing, "Show me thy ways, Lord" three times, and focus on your heart as the receptor for the answer to come through.

5. See curtains fall apart and truth rush in on waves of love, to be revealed a little at a time.

6. Upon opening your eyes, write your impressions under your question without mental interference.

7. For the next three days, watch for signs and intuitive images. For best results, always carry paper and pen to catch more. When your mind comes back to play havoc with your focus, send it off again, with love.

8. Repeat for three more days; review all clues and rewrite in new words what has been revealed.

## A contemplative exercise with a mantra that extends longevity and life understanding

As above, do a similar exercise asking for life extension and greater understanding.

1. Write your concern or question (one at a time would be less confusing) on the top of a blank page and again, ask the Inner Master for guidance.

2. Sing, "Heal my heart, my God!" three to six times.

3. As above, ask your mind to do research on the topic. You can envision going to a Golden or Blue Library of Light upon the Earth or Inner Worlds. Let go of all worries or concerns.

4. When awake, you may randomly search the Internet, library, or other written, audio, or video material for answers.

5. Let soul, heart, and your intuitive senses guide you and let answers pop out like popcorn that need to be jotted down.

6. Be sure to keep notes, because what seems obvious and unimportant in one moment could become an important connecting thread which might otherwise be lost.

(continued next page)

7. Ask your mind for the results of its research upon its return; write what comes to you and contemplate on it. If you truly do this from soul consciousness in willing alignment with God, there is no limit to what you may discover.

♥ ♥ ♥

# Chapter Eleven

## The Role of the Spiritual Temples of Wisdom

♥ ♥ ♥

*Their collective mission is to balance the encroaching Kali Yuga and increasingly menacing dark forces, and refocus souls and modern civilization on the heart center and the giving of unconditional love at all times under all circumstances, while providing needed tools to accomplish this vital task.*

♥ ♥ ♥

## Why the spiritual hierarchies constructed spiritual temples on the lower and upper worlds of this universe

Spiritual hierarchies constructed numerous spiritual temples on the lower and upper worlds of this universe because they needed specific places to meet and train together and pass knowledge and wisdom to aspiring students who would become spiritual masters in the future. These temples became hot spots of energy, vortices connecting plane to plane from Sugmad to an established or forming collective consciousness, then connecting individual masters to individual souls. The spiritual hierarchies need to use an orderly step down of energy vibration for experience, expansion, and contraction. Experimental vortices created in various places helped souls learn the use of Universal Soul Movement, soul and mental exploration, the use of creative principles, and manifestation for other souls to gain and benefit. Once souls began to develop higher consciousness, the social consciousness of an incarnated culture and its limited creations and toys no longer held advanced souls' interest. Since souls are very creative by nature, they need to constantly have access to places of higher learning or they will introvert and wreak havoc upon themselves and their neighbors.

## Why "Universal Soul Movement" is a direct means of traveling to the spiritual temples

Contemplation is focused attention of the lower dual world bodies, which includes the physical, astral, causal, and mental. Universal Soul Movement is focused movement or conscious expansion of soul and can be done in all the lower and higher worlds. It is limited only by the restrictions the individual places upon him or herself. Daily practice of , 149Universal Soul Movement is the only way to align all parts and facets of the individual and focus on the energy vortices. How else could souls travel to the Inner temples except by Universal Soul Movement? The physical body cannot leave the Physical Plane. As above, so below: the astral body cannot rise above the Astral Plane; the causal body and mental bodies also cannot move beyond their respective planes of existence. This is due to the construction of this Sugmad. However, souls alone are made in the image and likeness of Sugmad, and souls have the ability and the mandate to move and discover all of what they can be.

## Activities at these temples of wisdom

Some of the activities that happen at the Inner temples of wisdom are: purifications of engrams and advanced training in many areas, such as the imparting of secrets, learning ancient esoteric and arcane wisdom, how to handle increased love, how to gain and maintain increasing amounts of freedom, and how to handle increasing power and remain in perfect balance in order to succeed in the mission the soul has accepted. There is much more than what meets the eye, and mental awareness is needed to train souls into higher levels of vibratory frequencies and responsibilities.

## Why the masters of old prefer teaching their students at these temples

The masters of old knew that privacy would be vital to ensure safety in the arcane arts that would be damaged by insincere and malicious souls. They needed the ability to select, monitor and train students in a controlled environment, and quickly and thoroughly eliminate potentially damaging elements. Maintaining the purity of students is paramount, especially in personal integrity, purpose, and mission. The masters needed to create, maintain, and change or destroy any element that threatened their mission, as desired and needed for Best-Laid Plans. Few souls are invited; fewer pass the tests given over long periods of time.

## Why the spiritual city of Ekere Tere is located above Abuja, Nigeria

The spiritual city of Ekere Tere above Abuja, Nigeria was created at the request of Dan Rin and the Grand Council to galvanize the spiritual consciousness on Earth, to rebuild community, to refocus spiritual energies, and to be a primary channel for the vortex which comes from the highest planes of the pure God realms and moves through to the Physical Plane. The planet needs a new alignment, like a long awaited chiropractic adjustment. Africa needs renewed inflows of energies and advanced souls' attention focused on her renewal in order to gain a new status and to dissolve the millennia of destruction caused by a myriad of black magicians operating within its shores. A Spiritual Renaissance will come from the elimination of black magic and the restoration of the aligned vortices within Sugmad's Heart into the heart of Earth, which will bring fresh waves of the Light and Sound of Sugmad, and herald the counterbalance to the growing dark forces already present and proliferating. It is long past time to restore balance, as the dark forces have gained the upper hand and have not allowed the pure Light and Sound to penetrate into the Mental, Causal, and Astral Planes in proper balance. Souls need balanced energies to advance and flourish. Within the city of Ekere Tere, many masters will train advanced souls in many of their esoteric and practical arts. Souls will be able to take their next steps in purification, redirection, skill development, relaxation, and rejuvenation. Freedom from tyranny must come from this large and magnificent continent and its beautiful citizens, for Africa has symbolized the epitome of abuse and abject slavery of the worst kinds for far too long. This reputation is not fitting, for this continent is the mother and birthplace of human life.

## How these spiritual temples act as "worm-holes" and entrances to other parts of the universe

Spiritual temples actually contain (or are contained) within vortices of varying degrees of power that transform and transmit the highest frequencies as well as a range of frequencies coming from the highest realms into the location of the temple. Focus is required to bring a vortex into a level of beingness and focus is required of any soul endeavoring to enter a vortex or wormhole. A temple vortex shortens and condenses the distance between levels and similar places due to the magnitude of its energy and range; this allows travel by soul through what could be called a wormhole, a narrow pathway. Old concepts of movement through time and space are altered and elevated to a new consciousness. The old consciousness that is hardening to materialism is strangling souls' visions and needs replacement and a new face. These wormholes allow fast entry and exit by souls into realms previously unknown through an instant Universal Soul Movement paradigm. The techniques taught by Sri Michael and ascended Sehaji Masters can show a pure hearted soul the way into a temple, its vortex, and into another dimensions not previously accessible. The impossible and impassible become "do-able" in an instant with the master Oversoul leading the way through the maze of interconnecting energy vortices.

## The purpose of the spiritual city of Agam Des in Tibet

The spiritual city of Agam Des in Tibet exists to train souls on the Earth planet to achieve Universal Soul Movement and purity of thought, emotion, and action. Spiritual masters and initiates train qualified souls in a range of esoteric arts to reinvigorate the individual and collective consciousness to realign with Sugmad. The city maintains a spiritual vortex into the planet to keep the Earth consciousness from degenerating too fast into false truths and materialism. Ekere Tere assists Agam Des in its planetary mission as a new version for the inflowing of Spirit into a new set of people. Agam Des has existed for Tibetan Buddhists in Asia for eons and recently, within the last few centuries, has been opened to westerners of great merit. Ekere Tere was built for Africans, Europeans, and Americans who come to know of its origin, purpose, and location. Their collective mission is to balance the encroaching Kali Yuga and increasingly menacing dark forces, and refocus souls and modern civilization on the heart center and the giving of unconditional love at all times under all circumstances, while providing needed tools to accomplish this vital task.

## Why each spiritual temple has a guardian who oversees the daily affairs of the temple and screens those who seek to enter its gates

Each temple needs a guardian or an overseer to protect and monitor the mission and activities contained within its structure to maintain focus and purity at all times. The guardian must know the direction of the vortex so the correct spin will be sustained. This vital task requires a soul of great merit and training. He or she must keep movement within the vortex, and manage its flow and direction for joy, freedom, and accomplishment of certain missions. Each temple is also a unique focal point for the spiritual hierarchy to communicate its needs and desires if any changes are necessary. The guardian sets, sustains, and eliminates unwanted elements as directed by the spiritual hierarchy. The vital tasks of each temple and guardian include the creation, maintenance, and running of its assigned portions of the various planes, systems, forces, missions, tasks, and vibrations in all realms of the many universes of God. This is a tall order, one requiring a high degree of competence and loyalty to God's will and heart.

## Why the Spiritual Master Shams of Tabriz is located on the Causal Plane

Master Shams of Tabriz was the friend, companion, and teacher of the famous holy man and poet Rumi, from Turkey and Afghanistan in the $13^{th}$ century AD. Since Shams' departure as the Living Sehaji Master of his time, he has been guarding the main spiritual temple on the Causal Plane, which contains unconscious seed memories of past lives. It is a repository of the soul records of all souls, secured and stored for safekeeping. Soul can visit, and with Shams' permission and assistance, can read his or her own soul records for greater awareness and understanding of how life works and his or her individual place in the grand scheme. All this can be done, not for mere curiosity, but to resolve karma. One must have purity of mind and heart, vow and be able to keep the Law of Silence, especially regarding what might be revealed about other souls. If one wants to reveal information gained and risk contamination of one's own records and karma, then that is the right and responsibility of the individual soul. However, there are rules and spiritual principles which guarantee the rights of each soul. These laws must not be broken for risk of far ranging damage that might affect the collective consciousness and balance within the individual and interconnecting planes of existence. Souls must have demonstrated purity of heart and stamina of loyalty to their spiritual quests, as well as their willingness to adhere to God's mandates and wishes. Demonstration of loyalty and competence in spiritual matters are also essential to gain access. Once a trained soul screened by Shams is allowed entry, Shams will assign a mentor and will allow an accompanying master to direct or will show the visiting soul himself, the ways to answer questions the seeker has posed. The spiritual training to read soul records is generally long and rigorous, but the Living Sehaji Master or another Sehaji Master may grant grace in certain circumstances.

## The mission of the Katsupari Monastery under Spiritual Master Fubbi Quantz

The mission of the Katsupari Monastery under Fubbi Quantz serves as a way station for souls coming into and leaving the Earth plane and involves the training of souls in several areas: in the many duties, functions, and ways of life, in gracefully being able to transition from one phase of life to another, and in the freeing of soul to learn of its true nature beyond the confines of the human consciousness existing in the mass stream of daily life. Fubbi Quantz is an ancient master, with years far beyond what the mind would ordinarily conceive to be possible upon the Earth plane. He works directly with the newly departed souls who participate in and are trained in The Way of Truth. One of a spiritual seeker's advantages is that the Living Master personally intercedes with the Angel of Death and takes the newly departed of The Way of Truth into the Inner Worlds for his or her future assignment. This is greatly beneficial, as the soul in the presence of the Living Master is now able to bypass the Lords of Karma and is given a reprieve in his or her obligation to repay vast amounts of karma accumulated in the most recent as well as past lives. The soul is then introduced to Master Fubbi Quantz and given over to his temporary care to be trained to move on to his or her next phase of life with greater awareness, wisdom, love, responsibility, and freedom.

## A contemplative technique that will take the God seeker to the Causal Plane under Shams of Tabriz's direction to review his or her soul records

1. In a quiet safe place where you will be undisturbed for at least 30 to 60 minutes, settle into your body.

2. Breathe easily and focus on your heart center.

3. Ask the Living Master to guide you to the Causal Plane under Shams of Tabriz's direction to review your soul records. If you have a specific request in mind, write it down before beginning your Inner soul movement, and keep paper and pen close at hand to record your experience upon your safe return to your room.

4. Refocus on your heart and purest intention. Let go of any distractions.

5. Sing HU several times in a soft voice, and then sing **"SHO TE AUM."**

6. Focus on moving beyond the Astral Plane into the Inner Worlds and come to rest in a garden of great beauty.

7. Look around to experience the marvel of this place, and see a beautiful temple nearby. This is the place where memories of past and future lives are archived, called Akashic Records by many. The great River of God (that looks to many like a huge

waterfall rushing down from above) can be seen, bringing huge amounts of sparkling light, sound, and love into this plane from above.

8. Move up the stairs to the door of the golden temple building and meet the radiant master Shams.

9. He happily greets you and welcomes you into the temple.

10. As you move through the halls, notice the sights, sounds, feeling, and smells of this place.

11. You may be led to a room with books or screens, or simply move down long halls to see the answers to your query in the picture frames lining the walls or projected all around in holographic form. There are many ways to view your soul records.

12. Enjoy your experience; record it for your eyes only, and return for more experiences here as often as you feel called to do so.

## A contemplative technique that will give the God seeker the opportunity to see if there are segments of his or her life contract that can be changed

Do this technique after you have had at least several successes with the above exercise.

1. Focus on your heart.

2. Sing HU softly several times and then sing "**ALA SHANTU AUM.**"

3. Using Universal Soul Movement, see the garden and beautiful temple described above.

4. Meet with and ask Dan Rin and Shams whether segments of your life contract may be changed.

5. Open a dialogue. Honestly tell them what you want changed and why.

6. Listen carefully for their responses.

7. Remember that they are communicating with you whether their lips move or not, and whether you can consciously hear them or not.

8. Go with their guidance, stay focused and open, and record your experience, again for your eyes only.

♥ ♥ ♥

# Chapter Twelve

## The Way of Truth, a Path to God-Realization

♥ ♥ ♥

*The Way of Truth offers something quite unique and vital: it is both inter-dimensional and interdenominational. The Way of Truth offers a Living Master, who is the living embodiment of the Light and Sound of God, plus a description of and techniques to access many ascending states of spiritual awareness; these aspects are lacking for many God seekers along their other paths.*

♥ ♥ ♥

## Why some God seekers chose The Way of Truth as their Path to God-Realization

Many God seekers chose The Way of Truth as their Path to God-Realization because they have studied countless other paths with other teachers, including ascended teachers known in The Way of Truth, in this or past lifetimes. Whether the mind remembers it or not, soul learns from each experience. When souls have learned all they can and have ventured as far as they can go in their religion or spiritual path, they need a new teacher who can extend their training. Advanced souls who are ready to journey beyond Self-Realization need a spiritual teacher who has mastered God-Realization, if knowing and serving God is their goal. Many God seekers become participants of The Way of Truth when they have come to a place within their consciousness when they know that they are ready to take their next step along their journey into higher realms of beingness. When they are ready, willing, and able to do whatever it takes, they will have varying measures of success, in accordance with their states of consciousness. The Way of Truth offers something quite unique and vital: it is both inter-dimensional and interdenominational. The Way of Truth offers a Living Master, who is the living embodiment of the Light and Sound of God, plus a description of and techniques to access many ascending states of spiritual awareness; these aspects are lacking for many God seekers along their other paths. The training offered happens on both the Outer and Inner planes. All hungry souls are welcome to give new life and vitality to their religions, if they find forays into the Inner Worlds interesting and not threatening. Many leaders of various organized religions have studied with The Way of Truth to gain deeper insight into their own religions.

## The purpose of the Inner and Outer Teacher of The Way of Truth

The Outer Teacher of The Way of Truth, also known as the Living Sehaji Master, is currently Sri Michael Owens. All spiritual masters who have held this high level of responsibility have worn the mantle of the Rod of Power as mandated by the Grand Council, the executive body of the spiritual hierarchy that governs the worlds of Sugmad. The Outer Teacher is trained to handle the intense frequencies of the Inner Teacher, also known as the Inner Master, who is the focused consciousness of the Holy Spirit that works with souls in all the worlds. The Outer Teacher directly reflects the Inner Master Teacher and gives talks, writes discourses and books, answers initiates' reports, and carries on other duties as agreed upon with the Grand Council. The Inner Master is without form, but embodies the highest of Sugmad's consciousness. This high state of consciousness can be accessed by some souls who are advanced along the spiritual path and is available to all who call upon the Inner Master with a sincere and open heart.

## How the participants' understanding and spiritual stamina is increased by their relationship with the Inner Master

Participants love to drink of the pure spiritual waters of the Inner Master because it feels exquisite and bestows many benefits, both recognizable and far beyond the mind's ability to conceive. They rarely come to the Outer Master without having experienced the Inner Master in dreams or other openings into higher states of awareness. When participants call upon the Inner Master, it is generally for help in gaining something. Their understanding grows with an increasingly fine tuned awareness of the intense love and wisdom that pours into the heart and mind consciousness. As a participant studies life, personal responses, other's reactions to situations, and the application of lessons given, he or she broadens in subtle awareness, in self-awareness, and in soul awareness. Many of the lessons brought on by intensive spiritual study and alignment with the spiritual hierarchy also have the effect of changing the structure of the Inner bodies. As aberrations (which are Inner structures that block the flow of the Holy Spirit) are encountered, they need to be recognized, blessed, and purged. As the Inner bodies are purified and cleansed of the dross of this and past lives, increased spiritual energies rush in to fill the void left by the departure of these denser energies and blockages. Spiritual stamina is required and increased as participants follow the directions of the Outer and Inner Master and their bodies undergo changes and growth. Change is something that the emotional body and ego often finds uncomfortable and automatically rejects. Yet in The Way of Truth, the participants come to know that each stage of growth is also marked by expansion of understanding, stamina, wisdom, love, and freedom.

## What Self-Realization is and why it is a monumental step toward God-Realization

Self-Realization is a state of consciousness one moves through on the path toward God-Realization and beyond. In this state, soul knows that its identity is soul, not the lower bodies that soul inhabits to gain experience in various levels of beingness. Most people on Earth think they are their physical body; some identify the self as the mind or the emotions. Self-Realization is a monumental step toward God-Realization, in which soul recognizes its relationship with God. Only in these states of higher consciousness can soul understand not only his or her true nature, but also the nature of all reality. Self-Realization requires much refinement and training and is offered only by the Inner and Outer Master.

## The spiritual virtues God seekers must develop in their trek to God-Realization

God seekers must develop many spiritual virtues. First and foremost, the seekers must learn to stay open and focused on the heart center at all times, surrendering to the flow of the Love and Light and Sound of God. God emits pure Unconditional Love, so if the seeker wishes to channel the God energies, he or she must be prepared and committed to continually remain open to the flow of increasingly stronger God energies in order to accomplish Sugmad's goals. Awareness of the process is essential. The seeker must awaken to and accept truth, realign with the proper flow of Spirit, and remain in balance for the God energies to use him or her as It sees fit. The seeker must be willing to give up many former treasures: anger, bitterness, grudges, attachments to material gain, vanity, greed, the ego, self-will, boastfulness, the need to be acknowledged and admired, depression, mental conceptions reflecting the social consciousness, wrong thinking, connections with the dark forces, and other habits that hinder the flow of Spirit. The seeker must learn to create his or her unique place in the grand scheme of forces that are totally beyond the mind's ken. The God seeker must learn to master the Law of Silence in matters of spiritual importance in order to understand without interruption and learn to handle the increased God energies coming in to the bodies. Self-Realization is a needed step along the path. Giving to others without thought of reward refines the soul and allows the Inner bodies to shine with the glory of God. Listening to the Inner nudges of the Inner Teacher and other Inner Masters of the Grand Council and acting, without reservation, upon the spiritual directions given, becomes vital. Many God seekers are placed under rigorous training as they grow toward becoming a member of the spiritual hierarchy and work as team members without resistance to the directions imparted. Such spiritual training is a privilege and an essential task.

## Why the attainment of God-Realization breaks the wheel of reincarnation

Souls are bound to the wheel of reincarnation through adherence to the mind, the dictates of the social consciousness, and ignorance of the spiritual laws and truths that govern existence. God-Realization breaks the wheel of reincarnation when soul is able to live in the true Light and Sound - the intense love and energetic frequencies of God. The attainment of Self-Realization marks the beginning of soul's true journey into realms unimaginable by the mind. The attainment of God-Realization continues that ecstatic journey into the heart and mind of God and far beyond. This is inconceivable to the mental consciousness of today, but it contains a set of experiences that Spirit's current pioneers are beginning to experience. The realms of God are infinite. Soul must leave the Earth world altogether in order to explore many of the farthest realms; achieving the state of consciousness known as God-Realization is the breaking point for the need to return to Earth for soul's individual lessons and repayment of debts. However, souls may choose or may be assigned to reincarnate to lead others along the path to this high spiritual state.

## The meaning of God-Realization and how it affects the personality and character of the God seeker

God-Realization is a point of perfect balance in the heart of the entity known as Sugmad. It is the beginning and ending of all existence and energetic resonance in this sphere of existence. Since Unconditional Love for all life is a central defining feature of Its heart, the personality and character of the God seeker also transforms into pure unconditional love. A God seeker who lives in this exalted state loves and respects other souls in ways seemingly incomprehensible to the normal human consciousness. A God-Realized soul gives love in every situation, regardless of his or her personal emotional condition. He or she gives freedom to others to make whatever choices they need to make or are confined to make according to their life contracts. God-Realized souls' characters are composed of the highest ethics, since hurting another or deterring them from their chosen path is forbidden. Personal sacrifices for the good of the whole are common, but God-Realized beings also know how to protect themselves and their personal and collective missions, which are paramount to their lives and the common good. God-Realized individuals are no longer interested in only their own welfare, for the welfare of their entire nation and global community becomes their primary focus. They treasure personal pleasure and enjoyment, but even more, they gain great pleasure in seeing the happiness of others, and they are willing and eager to sacrifice immediate gratification for the greater goals and good. The God seeker has at last become the God giver, for he or she can now give and receive in balanced measure and takes the greatest pleasure in the opening of the hearts of others. Gone are interests of personal recognition. God-Realized souls tend to be quiet, modest, self-effacing, unassuming, balanced, and poised in humility and total surrender to the greatest of God energies. You can recognize them by their quiet and gentle, but powerful strength of character and demeanor.

## Why the consistent daily practice of the contemplative exercises is a direct doorway to God-Realization

Consistent daily practice of the contemplative exercises provided by the Living Sehaji Master is a direct doorway to the opening of the heart and the flowering of the personality common to the state of consciousness of God-Realization. How else can the mind and emotions steeped in the rigors of daily life be overcome and balanced with the opposing forces of the Heart of God? Earthly life and the Heart of God are polar opposites in many respects. Daily contemplative practices cleanse and refresh the Inner bodies like a warm shower cleanses the Outer body and establish a rhythm and routine to enlarge the capabilities of the Inner bodies to handle increasing God energies and viewpoints. Daily spiritual practice gently opens blockages that inhibit the God flow and makes it easier to remain in balance when the direction of the seeker's course needs to be corrected. Regular contemplation allows the individual to regain spiritual balance daily and gain stamina and maturity as he or she moves along his or her journey from ignorance and misery to total awareness and joy.

## Why the heart is a conduit of the God Power and the communication line of the God Worlds

The heart is the instrument attuned to the melody of love sent from the Heart of God. The mind is designed for other purposes; the mind's limitations prevent it from seeing clearly, as it is steeped in analysis and ego protecting traits. Each organ of the physical body serves a purpose for the good of the whole organism, in a physical and psychic sense. The heart is the central pump and station for circulating energies on all levels of existence. It is through the unique capabilities of the heart that the individual can focus and communicate with other beings in realms within and beyond the mind. This is the expressed design of the Sugmad, not a random meaningless by-product of chaos. The heart is the conduit of the God power. As soul learns to put attention on the heart in all its activities and as soul connects heart-to-heart with others in pure intention, heart and soul become a great conduit for the God power. Lines of communication then open within the God Worlds beyond their previous awareness and capacities. The heart is built for love, connection, commitment and communication.

## The spiritual importance of The Way of Truth's Holy Books I & II being completed by the end of 2008

Many world changes are progressing to bring down the consciousness of the Earth world into greater power, greed, and materialism. This rapid decline in consciousness needs to be balanced with strong channels and vortices of Light and Sound of the highest order. The presence of the strong leadership of many God-Realized souls at work in a myriad of functions is essential to counter the encroaching dark powers. *The Way of Truth Eternal - Books I and II* (Holy Books I and II) must be completed and widely distributed as soon as humanly possible in order to help train eager souls to climb the spiritual ladder with greater clarity and speed than ever before needed. These Holy Books are filled with wisdom that the mind can grasp and use to progress along the spiritual path to the Heart of God, also known as the Sea of Love and Mercy. More importantly, the master vibration of the books speaks directly to the heart and soul of God seekers. Whosoever shall pick up these books with sincerity, humility, and willingness will be transformed by merely holding them and contemplating their many messages of hope and practical techniques, which were designed to move the God seeker beyond the known edges of consciousness. Time is now of the essence, for the sake of balance.

## A contemplative technique with a mantra that will allow the participant the opportunity of viewing the Sea of Love and Mercy

The God seeker may visit and view the great Sea of Love and Mercy by learning to negotiate the subtle distinctive levels of vibrating energetic frequencies emitted in the various levels of God. The seeker must learn how to move from coarser to finer vibrations and learn how to develop great stamina in order to integrate the various levels into his or her consciousness.

1. To begin this integration process and view the great Sea of God, one should sit quietly and undisturbed for at least 30-60 minutes. Place your attention on the heart center.

2. Feel the love God has for you, listen with silent ears to the beating of the heart, and call to the Inner Master.

3. Ask him to come and guide you from the place where you sit, out of the physical body, through the various levels of finer vibration, and into the $14^{th}$ plane, where dwells the Great Spiritual Ocean.

4. Sing **"SUGMAD, BRING ME HOME."**

5. Feel yourself rise slowly and steadily through your physical body, then your emotional body, then your memory banks of the unconscious mind, then the vast clarity of the mental worlds, and finally through the intuitive functioning of the Etheric Plane.

6. You will then cross the barrier to the Soul Plane and then move upward and inward through successively finer levels of beingness. You do not need to know how to do this "properly," and do not wonder if you are doing this right, for to ponder these aspects is to lose any benefit gained from surrendering to this process. Allow the Inner Master to take you. Hold the goal lightly in mind and surrender.

7. Whenever you see the Light of God and hear the beautiful music as it changes in each succeeding plane, keep going. It is important to keep your imagination moving toward a higher love and Light and Sound. Soul will know when you have arrived, but the mind will think that the first plane of brilliant Light and Sound is heaven, the home of God. This is not true. God's true home is far beyond. You must trust that what you get is where you need to be for now.

8. Keep practicing and watch your Inner worlds expand and your experiences grow in a most loving way. Take the time to do this repeatedly.

## A contemplative technique that will give the participant a glimpse of God-Realization

1. Go into quiet contemplation and ask the Inner Master for a glimpse of God- Realization. Quietly within your own heart, envision a golden white light glowing, gaining in strength and momentum, flying out in all directions with the strength and force of a mother's love for her child.

2. Sing "**HU ALAYHA**" for a few moments. You are a child of Sugmad.

3. Envision and feel the more powerful love of God, your parent, gently connecting to your heart, and as you rejoin in full consciousness, thank the God who gives you continual life for the blessings bestowed upon you each day. Bless all inside you, all outside you, as you and God merge into an infinite golden globe of universal absorption.

♥ ♥ ♥

*Blessed Be!*

*For more information, you are invited to visit:*

*www.thewayoftruth.org on the world wide web.*

♥ ♥ ♥

# Index

## A

## B



## C

## D



## E

(Continued)

## *H*

## J



## K



## L

## N



## O

## *Q*



## *R*

(Continued)

## T

## W



## X (none)

## Y



## Z (none)

# *Glossary*

## *A*

**Astral Plane** The Astral Plane, also called the emotional plane, is the powerhouse for physical movement. A more sensitive transformer of the higher energies than the physical body, the plane is also the realm of the emotions.

## *B*

**Best-Laid-Plans** Sugmad's dream for its creation of the universe and all life forms; a dream in which sleeping souls tested, tried and proven through the fires of purification, eventually awaken. Once fully awake, Sugmad's children see each other as brother and sister, person to person, nation to nation. Love, peace, harmony and Sugmad's abundance reign.

## *C*

**Causal Plane** The Causal Plane was created as a storehouse for memory to be accessible for the use of soul in any of the lower worlds.

**Charity** Charity is a gift of love with no strings attached.

**Contemplation** This is an active form of engaging the mind in activity aligned with soul, and in this way, differs from prayer and meditation.

## *D (none)*

## *E*

**Ego** A part of the mind, ego's purpose is survival. Too often seduced by power, in actuality, the ego is like a ping pong ball when compared to the sun.

**Etheric Plane** The Etheric Plane sits just below the Soul Plane, is the highest region of the Mental Plane, and was created to begin soul's descent into the Lower Worlds.

## *F (none)*

## *G*

**God-Absorption** Involves seeing, knowing and being a son or daughter of Sugmad. It is the ultimate reunification with Sugmad such that when you move, Sugmad moves.

**God-Realization** The cellular recognition, ignited from within, that you are a part of God.

## *H*

**HU** HU is the sacred gift from this Sugmad to the souls of this universe who are ready to receive the heart of its truth.; As the final key to the highest plane in the long journey through all the lower realms of this universe back to the heart of God, it can open every door. Use the HU to seek the destination of your heart.

## *I*

**Initiations** Initiations acknowledge souls passing tests on their journey home to the heart of Sugmad. They provide structure and catapult soul to new uncharted territory in each successive plane of its journey.

## *J (none)*

## *K*

**Kal Niranjan** Kal Niranjan was designated by Sugmad as Lord of the Lower Planes. Kal is not malicious or vicious as he has been portrayed. He merely carries out his assigned duties with precision and deft artistry.

**Karma** Also known as the Law of Cause and Effect, karma is the law by which soul reaps the rewards or experiences the consequences of prior actions, even from past lives, whether soul remembers them or not.

## *L*

**Law of Compassion** This Law allows soul a way to give love under any circumstances.

**Law of Freedom** Freedom creates, contains and maintains the vital energies of life. This Law enables Sugmad to learn of Its true and full potential.

**Law of Noninterference** This Law renders respect to all life. This is accord with Sugmad's gift of free will to all souls, and allows souls to evolve in their own unique ways.

**Law of Silence** Little understood but greatly needed, silence is pregnant with power. Silence holds great energetic frequencies of the Light and Sound.

**Law of Unity** This Law is a reminder that our true goal and state is union with Sugmad and one another.

**Life Contract** A life contract specifies a mission; it gives direction as an agreement to move in certain areas to gain awareness and expertise unique to self in relation to others to fulfill a greater purpose.

**Light and Sound** These are the primary emanations from Sugmad that constitute the Life Force, source of all life and All That Is.

**Love** Love is the essential nature of Sugmad, soul, and all manifestation. Love creates and sustains our universe; the absence of love destroys.

## *M*

**Mental Plane** The mental realm or mind without physical brain stuff, was made to take the intuitive impulses and step them down a few notches more. The Mental Plane includes the Etheric, however, the Etheric is of a higher vibratory quality and sits directly below the Soul Plane.

## *N*

**Non-power** The non-power is the receiver, the receptacle of Sugmad's Power. To experience the non-power, one must achieve true detachment with full loving awareness.

## *O (none)*

## *P*

**Physical Plane** The Physical Plane was created for souls to experience gross and corporeal beauty and pain from its sensory apparatus. As the lowest Plane, it completes Sugmad's playground and grand experiment for the education and evolution of souls, sparks of Sugmad's own Self, units of Sugmad's awareness.

## *Q (none)*

## *R (none)*

## *S*

**Self-Realization** This is the first stage of soul's entrance into the heavenly worlds as it journeys into these worlds on beingness and pure love. Here the aspirant recognizes her or himself as Soul, not as the lower bodies soul uses to gain experiences in the Lower Worlds.

**Soul** Soul is a part of God, "made in His image" and is actually the same in nature as Sugmad.

**Sugmad** This constitutes a pure name for God, the Creator of this universe and all life forms.

## *T*

**Temples of Wisdom** These are Inner Temples where spiritual training, purification and the imparting of secrets occur. These spiritual temples are contained within vortices of varying degrees that transmit frequencies coming from the highest realms.

## *U*

**Universal Laws** Sugmad established universal laws to bring order into consciousness from chaos. Like a train track for trains, or the Internet for ideas, universal laws provide a structure for creation and manifestation.

## *V (none)*

## *W (none)*

## *X (none)*

## *Y (none)*

## *Z (none)*

# Other Books by Michael Edward Owens

(Sri Michael Owens)

♥ ♥ ♥

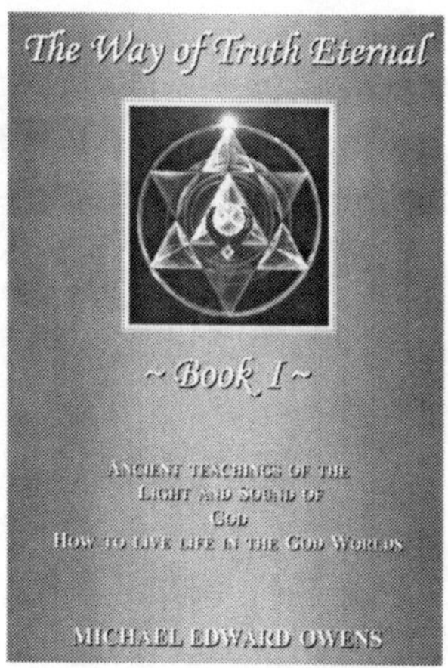


## *The Way of Truth Eternal ~ Book I*

The ancient words of truth are written in the sacred pages of the Holy Books of the Light and Sound. These sacred writings are contained and housed and held and protected in sacred temples of light where they are guarded by the members of the Sehaji Hierarchies. As the universe unfolds and progresses, these works are given and revealed in physical form below to create a grounding point for the vortex of their energy and power so that it might be found and felt and experienced within the realms where it is needed.

And so, this is the first of these luminous works given to man by the hand of the Sehaji, Dan Rin, the current Living Sehaji Master, and its words and truth are vital because they do address of critical points of confluence, which previously had been blocked and obstructed and had prevented the clear flows of energy that are necessary and required by those groups of Souls currently incarnated on Earth and within the other realms and seeking in their progression to move together onward on the path.

And so, *The Way of Truth Eternal, Book I* has been sent and given to all Souls to open up their hearts and to aid their understanding and their movement on the path and return to higher realms above.

*Sri Michael Owens*

## Babaji, The Beginning Has No End

It is my privilege and pleasure to write this introduction on the dialogues of Babaji. I have admired this great avatar throughout my many lifetimes. He has been a dear friend and mentor whose help has been invaluable in my leadership of the path of Light and Sound, The Way of Truth. Babaji taught me how to examine and use the chakras in the movement of consciousness outside the body called, "Universal Soul Movement."

Babaji also initiated the awakening of my spiritual training in the physical realms. It was this great avatar that introduced me to my later mentors and teachers of old: Kadmon, Agnotti, and Milati. These spiritual masters have been my advisors since the beginning of my spiritual journey.

It was Babaji's intention to give those who know and love him a book that provides creative responses to the issues of love, family, work and daily life. Consequently, this book discusses spirituality in a way unique to other books on Babaji. What I found extremely effective for daily living were the contemplative exercises he offers in this book to expand the God seeker's sphere of love and knowledge. The words used as mantras (words of prayer) are phonetically charged with love and Light and Sound. The meaning of certain phraseology in the contemplative exercises is written to transcend the intervention of the mind. I have used terminology entrenched in the olden ways of the spiritual, like Sugmad, also known as God. This term was used due to its structural integrity, and it has never been profaned in human language and verbal communication. Thus, the vibration to the word "Sugmad" has never been depleted or violated.

As the Living Teacher of The Way of Truth, I am called a Sehaji Master. The term "Sehaji" means, "Master of the Celestial Seas," alluding to the Great Sea of Love and Mercy, the home of God's consciousness. This book was not intended to recruit or to propagandize the teachings of The Way of Truth, but there are references made to it throughout this book. Babaji's spiritual teachings and those of The Way of Truth were inevitable to intersect with one another. In essence, the foundations of both ways of life are integrally related to the beauty of God's love for all life and the freedom of Soul.

I believe you will find this book spiritually uplifting and of practical use in matters of spiritual inquiry. Many doors of perception and adventure await the God seeker who reads this book, uses the contemplative exercises, and follows the path inside this book. The truth unveiled in this book is like the light shining brightly at the end of the tunnel.

*Sri Michael Owens*

## *Ekere Tere, City of Light*

This book is a compilation of my spiritual studies with various teachers who are now teaching at Ekere Tere, the City of Light. This city was constructed in the High Astral Plane above the capital city of Abuja, Nigeria. Ekere Tere is a place of learning, specifically designed to forefront the newly calibrated teachings of The Way of Truth, to eradicate the imbalanced presence of black magic in the world and to open the spiritual doors of Africa's Renaissance.

The Way of Truth, the new path of the Light and Sound, stands as the spiritual guardian of all ways of life through the higher learning of Ekere Tere, the City of Light. The Way of Truth affirms the vibratory essence of the Light and Sound in every theology and life-path that holds unconditional love and non-judgment as its foundation. The unitary consciousness of all life is cohesively welded together by Sugmad's love and it is this love which is serving all life as the driving force of existence. It is our heart and its ability to connect with the eternal fabric of Sugmad's plan that opens our Universal Soul Movement to the inexplicable bliss beyond the ken of human eyes. Our heart is the key.

There are many paths to God and each soul must choose the course of their own spiritual unfoldment. This is Soul's eternal right. Soul was placed in a physical shell to understand its immortal gift of existence and to learn in a human laboratory of communication and cooperation, and ultimately to expand its consciousness of love and begin its Universal Soul Movement home.

Within the contents of this book, there is spoken dialogue which presents limitless knowledge to the seekers who want God-Realization in this lifetime. The spoken word of these Masters gives the reader a great opportunity to partake of the love I felt throughout the years of my spiritual training. It is my hope you will try the spiritual exercises to see if they fulfill your spiritual needs. To those seeking to see and visit Ekere Tere, you have my love and Darshan. A great adventure awaits each of you.

Many Blessings,

*Sri Michael Owens*

♥ ♥ ♥

Notes

♥ ♥ ♥

♥ ♥ ♥

Notes

Notes

♥ ♥ ♥

Notes

♥ ♥ ♥

♥ ♥ ♥

## Notes

♥ ♥ ♥

♥ ♥ ♥

Notes

♥ ♥ ♥

Notes

♥ ♥ ♥

Notes

♥ ♥ ♥

Made in the USA